A March Towards TYRANNY

Society's Steady Decline Into Authoritarian Rule

By: J. R. Moody

A very special thanks

to my oldest friend, Joey D.,

Who kept believing in me,

when everyone else, including myself, gave up.

Thank you, my friend!

TABLE OF CONTENTS

Introduction

Unveiling the Shadow: The Global Shift to Authoritarianism

The digital era promised a world where everyone could connect freely and share ideas without borders. However, this bright vision is overshadowed by a reality where information flow is tightly controlled by those in power. As governments across the world increase their grip on the internet, the effects on personal freedom and privacy are becoming alarmingly evident. This shift is redefining our interaction with the digital world, posing serious questions about our rights online.

At the core of this issue is a significant increase in government surveillance and censorship. This move towards authoritarian practices not only affects the digital realm but also threatens the foundational principles of democracy. People find themselves under constant watch, with every action online being tracked and potentially held against them. This atmosphere of fear leads to self-censorship, undermining the essence of open societies by suppressing dissent and dulling the lively exchange of ideas. This isn't an isolated problem; it's a worldwide concern that impacts civil liberties and the stability of democracies all over.

Authoritarian governments are leaning into advanced technology to solidify their control, often sacrificing individual freedom and privacy in the process. The rise of artificial intelligence (AI) has handed these regimes powerful tools to watch over citizens and twist the online narrative. For example, they're using generative AI to craft deepfakes and false stories that shake people's faith in democracy. Even when these tactics are uncovered, they significantly damage the quality of public discourse, leading journalists and activists to censor themselves and overshadowing trustworthy news.

Furthermore, the embrace of Key Internet Controls shows a move toward subtler, more concealed censorship methods. These governments place legal and technical boundaries on the digital realm to indirectly block access to unfiltered information. This strategy not only centralizes power but also isolates citizens from global conversations, creating an internet that varies dramatically based on where you live and the whims of those in charge.

At the heart of this dilemma is the clash between authoritarian internet governance, which seeks control and order, and an open approach that champions free speech and information access. Nations such as China and Russia are at the forefront of advocating for cyber sovereignty, pushing the idea that each country should control its digital domain as it sees fit. This stance risks fracturing the internet along national lines, undermining its foundation as a platform for free exchange and innovation.

Yet, there's a glimmer of hope. Actions against digital suppression and the battle against internet fragmentation are picking up speed. Democracies, through frameworks like the Summit for Democracy and the Declaration for the Future of the Internet, are striving to uphold the ideals of an accessible and secure worldwide web. These efforts lay down markers for safeguarding online freedoms and counter the shaping of the digital realm by authoritarian powers.

Addressing these issues demands a balanced strategy. Protecting privacy and data in this age of widespread surveillance is crucial. Regulations such as the EU's General Data Protection Regulation (GDPR) mark significant progress in defending online rights. However, it's also critical to ensure these laws don't split the internet further or hinder information sharing across borders. A global effort to align data protection standards could offset such concerns, promoting an internet that supports both privacy and openness.

The struggle with authoritarian encroachment online isn't solely about policy. It's about enabling individuals and communities to stand up for their digital rights. Backing technologies that bypass restrictions, bolstering independent media, and boosting digital know-how are all essential in creating an internet resilient to authoritarian sway.

The path forward requires dialogue and teamwork among nations, tech firms, civic groups, and international bodies. United by a commitment to liberty and democratic values, we can aim to keep the internet a positive force globally.

Reflecting on these points, it's clear that the struggle for control of the internet represents a larger conflict between authoritarianism and democracy. The result of this battle will not only impact our digital spaces but also the fundamental fabric of global society. For those committed to upholding personal freedoms and the welfare of all, participating in this fight with a focus on facts and human values rather than technology or politics is essential.

The Personal Toll: Living under the Watchful Eye

The growing influence of authoritarianism worldwide signals more than just a change in politics or ideology. It hits much closer to home, impacting the very core of society and our fundamental rights to freedom and privacy. Various tactics, including mass censorship, privacy breaches, and constant surveillance by governments, are infringing upon citizens' freedoms at an alarming pace, creating an environment filled with fear and anxiety. This atmosphere stifles free speech and erodes the liberties individuals once took for granted.

It's essential to grasp the emotional and psychological toll these government overreaches have on people. The harm isn't merely in the actions themselves but also in how they linger in people's minds and affect communities as a whole. The awareness that one's every move, online or offline, could be under scrutiny leads many to self-censor, holding back their true thoughts out of fear of retaliation or monitoring by authorities.

The reluctance to speak openly brings to mind the oppressive regime seen in Orwell's "1984," where constant surveillance by Big Brother crushes any opposition or individuality. The similarity between this fictional portrayal and our present reality emphasizes the seriousness of these issues. As voices are silenced, the core of democracy itself—active public discourse and dialogue—is undermined.

Furthermore, widespread surveillance and censorship not only silence opposition but also sow seeds of distrust among communities and towards those in power. People begin doubting their peers, questioning the confidentiality of their private discussions. This breakdown of trust affects more than just the political sphere; it infiltrates the social connections, putting a strain on personal relationships and community solidarity.

Recognizing the extent of these problems is a critical step towards addressing them. Fighting against authoritarian practices involves more than just bringing back privacy or ending censorship. It's about mending communities and restoring the eroded trust. Tackling these deep-rooted fears and concerns demands a thoughtful approach, combining policy changes with efforts to rebuild public confidence in protective systems.

One initial step towards recovery is enhancing transparency and accountability in government operations. Citizens must feel confident that their rights are protected, not infringed upon. Establishing strong legal protections for individual freedoms is crucial. But beyond legislation, fostering an open dialogue between the public and authorities, and encouraging active participation in governance, is equally important.

Confronting these challenges is no simple task. It involves addressing difficult questions about balancing security with freedom, the role of technology in surveillance, and establishing institutions resilient to authoritarian tendencies. Drawing wisdom from academic research and real-world events is crucial in navigating these challenges.

Hinckley and Harell delve into how authoritarianism in North America can be fueled by selectively consuming specific types of information. Their research uncovers that individuals inclined towards authoritarianism tend to avoid content supporting civil liberties, opting instead for material affirming their current beliefs. This pattern of selective information intake contributes to a divided society where conflicting viewpoints struggle to coexist. Recognizing these behaviors is crucial for devising approaches that foster exposure to diverse perspectives, encouraging tolerance and mutual understanding.

At the center of resisting authoritarianism is the unwavering importance of civil liberties and individual freedoms. In our fight against authoritarian tendencies, it's crucial to remember these core values. Crafting laws and policies to protect privacy and freedom of expression must be done carefully to avoid undermining the freedoms they aim to safeguard.

The fight against these infringements on our rights goes beyond mere policy adjustments; it is essentially a battle for the core values of democracy and basic human rights. Tackling these issues demands a unified effort worldwide from governments, Big Tech companies, civic organizations, and individuals alike. Although legal frameworks like the

GDPR represent progress, they are only initial steps in protecting our online liberties without breaking up the internet or hindering the free exchange of information.

Chapter 1

The Rise of Authoritarian Rule

Throughout history, it's been observed that oppressive rulers and regimes often start to appear when a society begins to step away from democratic values. This slow move away from democratic traditions is a critical signal pointing to a deeper problem—it shows us that authoritarianism doesn't just pop up out of nowhere. It's the result of weakening legal systems and community standards. By paying attention to early signs, like divisive speech and twisting the laws to one's benefit, we can spot the warning signs of a country inching towards authoritarian rule. Understanding these early shifts is key to pinpointing when democracies are in danger, setting the stage for a richer investigation into how authoritarian leaders manage to take and hold power.

The rise of authoritarian leaders is often tied to deep societal divisions and economic disparities. These issues do more than cause tension; they create a setting where leaders promising quick fixes seem highly appealing. Unfortunately, these hasty solutions typically come at the expense of democratic values and the fundamental principles that safeguard freedom and equality. The appeal of simplistic responses to complex issues underlines the challenges confronting democracies today. It underscores the necessity of exploring how economic and social disruptions erode democratic structures, offering a holistic perspective on this complex issue without resorting to oversimplified explanations or overlooking the complexities of political and social dynamics.

Subtle changes, like the rise of polarizing language that erodes trust in democratic institutions or the manipulation of laws to centralize power, signal more than just political swings—they may very well be the early warnings of a darker turn towards dictatorship.

The gap between the rich and the poor, along with social divisions, play a significant role in weakening democracies. When people feel neglected or disadvantaged because of economic struggles, they might be drawn to leaders who offer quick and radical fixes. These promises, though appealing because they offer hope of escape from financial and social problems, pose a danger. They threaten to dismantle the democratic structures meant to safeguard freedom and legal equality for everyone.

Understanding history's lessons on political turmoil is crucial. Democracies don't typically collapse overnight but deteriorate gradually, eroding norms and values bit by bit. This slow decay underscores the importance of remaining alert and remembering past mistakes. By recognizing early signs of trouble, communities can act to protect democratic values before irreversible damage is done.

Also essential is the protection of press freedom and an independent judiciary. These pillars of democracy serve as safeguards against excessive power, keeping government actions transparent and information flow unhindered. Attacks on these institutions pave a smoother path for authoritarianism, as they hamper the public's ability to critically evaluate governmental policies and actions.

To fend off authoritarian tendencies, being aware of history and societal weaknesses is key. Such awareness fosters resilience against the temptation of authoritarian solutions to intricate challenges. Cultivating this resilience involves both education about democracy and active participation in democratic processes at every level of society.

Democracy should be seen not as something simply handed down through generations but as an ongoing practice that needs care and active involvement. Encouraging people to take part in local politics, promoting open and civil discussions, and demanding transparency and responsibility from leaders are all vital steps.

The core of the fight against authoritarianism centers on championing fairness and justice. Authoritarian leaders often exploit valid grievances rooted in economic inequalities and social injustices. Therefore, addressing these fundamental issues transcends mere social policy; it serves as a pivotal component in safeguarding and enhancing democratic governance.

Exploitation of Societal Fears by Authoritarian Leaders

Authoritarian leaders have a knack for tapping into society's fears and insecurities. It starts with understanding that fear, a basic human reaction to threats, can make people act irrationally, often turning to leaders who promise safety yet may undermine individual rights in the process. Fear's power lies in its ability to cloud judgment, enforce conformity, and silence opposition. To push back against this, it's important for people to reflect on their fears, critically evaluate the solutions offered by those in authority, and not just accept them at face value.

Furthermore, propaganda plays a significant role in molding public opinion. Authoritarian governments are skilled in spinning tales of exaggerated dangers, both from within and abroad, casting themselves as the saviors. They create the problem, in order to sell us the solution. This constant bombardment with fear-driven messages distorts how people see the world, making the leader's protective role seem larger than life.

Authoritarian leaders tend to capitalize on crises to gain more authority quickly. Whether the crisis is genuine or fabricated, these figures see it as an opportunity to consolidate power. In times of uncertainty, their focus shifts towards solidifying control rather than prioritizing the protection of individual freedoms.

During emergencies, there is a noticeable decline in civil liberties as the general public's attention shifts towards restoring stability. This shift in focus often results in a diminishing emphasis on upholding democratic principles and oversight mechanisms. The urgency of the situation can lead to a temporary suspension of certain rights in the name of maintaining order.

Crises can pave the way for rapid changes in how governments exert their authority. Authoritarian figures may exploit the chaos of a crisis to implement policies that bolster their power and limit dissent. The population's immediate need for security and stability can create an environment conducive to the consolidation of control by authoritarian regimes.

During times of crisis, public discourse may shift from discussions about individual freedoms and civil rights towards conversations centered on security and survival. The heightened sense of vulnerability often prompts individuals to prioritize stability over challenges to government authority. This shift in priorities can enable authoritarian leaders to enact measures that curtail freedoms without significant opposition.

Crises introduce a level of uncertainty that authoritarian leaders can manipulate to enhance their authority. By presenting themselves as strong and decisive in the face of crisis, these leaders appeal to a populace seeking stability and security. The fear and confusion that accompany crises can create a conducive environment for authoritarian figures to increase their power base and influence over the population.

In times of crisis, oversight mechanisms and checks on governmental power may be temporarily set aside to expedite decision-making processes. The urgency of the situation often leads to a concentration of authority in the hands of a few individuals, weakening the systems designed to ensure governmental accountability. Authoritarian governments may use this disruption to consolidate their control without facing the usual constraints.

Crises can expose the fragility of democratic norms and institutions, particularly when leaders exploit emergency situations to expand their powers unchecked. The rapid erosion of civil liberties during crises highlights the vulnerability of democratic systems to authoritarian overreach. The public's immediate focus on stability can inadvertently contribute to the erosion of essential democratic principles.

Individuals may respond to authoritarian tactics during crises with a mixture of fear, compliance, and a desire for security. The threat of imminent danger can overshadow concerns about government overreach, prompting individuals to accept temporary limitations on their rights in exchange for perceived safety. Authoritarian governments use this fear and uncertainty to solidify their control and suppress dissent.

"Nothing is so permanent as a temporary government program" -Milton Friedman

The expansion of authoritarian control in response to crises can have lasting repercussions on society and governance. Temporary measures enacted during emergencies may become permanent, leading to a sustained erosion of civil liberties and democratic safeguards. The acceptance of increased government authority during crises can normalize authoritarian practices, setting a dangerous precedent for future governance.

The Patriot Act is a law that the U.S. government introduced after the 9/11 attacks. It aimed to enhance the government's ability to combat terrorism activities. The Act allowed the government to monitor communication channels, conduct surveillance on suspected individuals, and track financial transactions of potential terrorists. Initially, the Act was labeled as a temporary measure to deal with imminent threats.

As time passed, the temporary nature of the Patriot Act became less clear. The temporary removal of certain rights started to look more permanent. The provisions that initially seemed necessary in the face of a crisis became fixtures of American law. This transition blurred the lines between temporary security measures and long-term limitations on civil liberties.

The transition of the Patriot Act from a temporary response to a permanent fixture had far-reaching consequences on American citizens. The Act's provisions allowed for the collection of massive amounts of data on individuals, sometimes without transparent oversight or accountability. This raised concerns about privacy rights and the potential for abuse of power by government agencies.

One of the key aspects of the Patriot Act was its authorization of increased surveillance and monitoring activities. The government gained expanded authority to intercept communications, access personal records, and gather intelligence on suspected individuals. While these measures were deemed necessary for national security, they also raised questions about the extent of government intrusion into private lives.

The transition of the Patriot Act from a temporary solution to a permanent feature had implications for the checks and balances within the U.S. government. The Act granted significant powers to law enforcement and intelligence agencies, which could potentially circumvent traditional oversight mechanisms. This shift raised concerns about the concentration of authority and the erosion of accountability in matters of national security.

The evolving status of the Patriot Act sparked public debate and controversy. Some viewed the Act as a vital tool in safeguarding the nation against terrorist threats, while others raised alarms about its impact on civil liberties. The debate highlighted the tension between security and individual freedoms and underscored the complexities of balancing national security interests with constitutional rights.

Over the years, the Patriot Act faced legal challenges that questioned its constitutionality and the scope of government powers it conferred. Civil liberties advocates and concerned citizens challenged specific provisions of the Act in court, arguing that they infringed upon fundamental rights enshrined in the Constitution. These legal battles added another layer of complexity to the ongoing discourse surrounding the Act.

The transformation of the Patriot Act from a temporary response to a permanent fixture reflected the evolving security landscape in the post-9/11 era. The nature of threats to national security changed over time, leading policymakers to reassess the balance between security measures and individual freedoms. The Act's evolution mirrored broader shifts in how the government approached security challenges in a rapidly changing world.

As the Patriot Act shifted from a temporary measure to a lasting component of U.S. law, its long-term implications came into focus. The Act's provisions reshaped the relationship between security and privacy, government power and individual rights. The legacy of the Patriot Act served as a reminder of the complex trade-offs inherent in safeguarding the nation while upholding the principles of democracy and liberty.

This illuminates the challenges of addressing security threats in a democratic society. Its impact on civil liberties, government powers, and public discourse underscored the complexities of navigating security concerns in a world marked by uncertainty and rapid change. The evolution of the Patriot Act continues to shape ongoing debates about national security and individual rights in the United States.

It is Important to understand how leaders utilize crises for their benefit. Staying up to date with current events is one way to recognize when leaders might be taking advantage of a crisis. Learning from past instances where autocratic leaders have abused their power during emergencies is also key. During times of uncertainty, relying on independent media sources that provide unbiased information can help individuals understand the true nature of a crisis and how it is being manipulated by those in power.

Developing critical thinking and media savvy is essential in resisting authoritarian tactics. Cultivating a societal norm that prioritizes rational analysis over emotional reactions can help guard against fear-based manipulation. Dedicate time to learn and teach others about critical thinking and logical reasoning, diversify your news diet, focusing on independent media sources known for their accuracy and commitment to fact-checking, and engage in community conversations or online forums that promote discussion and idea sharing, challenging your viewpoints.

Understanding the use of psychological manipulation and propaganda is crucial for protecting democratic systems. As Freedom House points out, the spread of authoritarianism is a serious threat to liberty, marked by an assault on basic rights and efforts to weaken democratic standards. These insights emphasize the importance for democracies to proactively defend against the subtle encroachments of authoritarianism by identifying their strategies—such as exploiting fears, spreading misinformation, and capitalizing on crises—in order to prevent the erosion of freedoms.

Psychological Mechanics Behind Authoritarian Control

Understanding why authoritarian regimes appeal to some people requires more than just a look at politics. It takes a deep dive into human psychology to understand why certain groups may lean towards a system that values control and sameness over the freedom to be different and voice dissent. Central to this exploration is the idea that people are not solely driven by logic; our actions and beliefs are also shaped by our emotions, desires, and the innate longing for order and safety.

It's important to acknowledge the influence of social conformity and obedience in shaping how societies function. These traits aren't all bad, after all, they help build strong communities and predictable social interactions. Yet, it's precisely these aspects of human nature that authoritarian leaders manipulate to tighten their hold. The logic here is pretty straightforward: during uncertain times or when faced with threats, people crave leadership and clarity. This need can be twisted, leading folks to give up their freedoms for the promise of security and certainty.

The way power and authority psychology play out in authoritarian settings is key to understanding their persistence. Power here isn't just about enforcing rules but also about shaping what people see as truth or necessary. Leaders in such systems are really good at presenting themselves as the sole bearers of strength and stability, convincing others to follow them—not necessarily because they agree with them, but because of a deeply rooted yearning for order and safety.

Political divisions and a strong sense of 'us versus them' significantly heighten the risk of falling for authoritarian narratives. When society is fractured, and trust is low among different groups, authoritarian figures can pose as peacemakers. They use these rifts, often overstating threats from outside groups, to strengthen unity and loyalty within their own ranks. Creating an identity based on standing against perceived enemies can lead people to view authoritarian actions as justified defenses against both real and imagined dangers.

Battling these authoritarian inclinations means nurturing what's called a critical consciousness. This entails encouraging people to question official narratives, think independently, and critically evaluate political motives. To resist manipulation effectively, we must champion openness, encourage critical reflection, and promote empathy for different viewpoints. Education is incredibly important here, not just for sharing knowledge but for developing the capabilities needed for democratic participation and resisting authoritarian influences.

Understanding how authoritarian regimes manipulate people's weaknesses and group behaviors is crucial in defending against their influence. Being aware of how our psychology can be used against us forms the first line of defense. By recognizing these dynamics, we can establish stronger protections to safeguard democratic principles and institutions. It is vital to encourage a culture that values questioning and accountability to uphold a free and dynamic society.

Propaganda's Role in Consolidating Power

Grasping how propaganda and misinformation work is essential in today's world, which is more online than ever. Propaganda uses biased information to influence public opinion and solidify control, often seen in legacy mainstream media. Misinformation, though, spreads incorrect or misleading information by mistake, leading to misunderstandings without intending to mislead. These elements significantly shape what people believe and how they act, especially in authoritarian systems that depend on controlling the narrative.

When it comes to spreading propaganda and disinformation, certain tactics are employed to sway public perception. These methods include appealing to emotions, spreading untruths, and using distorted statistics, all aimed at skewing reality to fit a particular political goal. The success of these strategies often relies on tapping into existing prejudices or fears, blurring the line between what's real and what's not. Encouraging everyone to think critically, to doubt, and to scrutinize the source and aim of the information they encounter is important in resisting these manipulative efforts.

The phenomenon of echo chambers and filter bubbles makes battling misinformation even tougher by creating spaces where people only hear views that mirror their own. This situation restricts access to differing viewpoints, thereby cementing one-sided beliefs and fueling division. To break free from these constraints, making an effort to explore a range of news sources and engaging with opposing viewpoints is necessary. Such practices lead to a deeper understanding of topics, nurture empathy, and lessen societal divides.

In authoritarian states, controlling media and mass censorship are key tools for influencing public opinion. These governments manage the narrative to maintain power and suppress opposing opinions, hindering the free exchange of ideas and weakening democracy's foundations. Supporting independent journalism and the freedom of the internet stands out as vital defenses. Ensuring access to varied news outlets and the freedom to voice dissent without fear or censorship are fundamental for an informed populace and a robust democracy.

Teaching media literacy and supporting fact-checking are effective measures against propaganda's influence. Educating people on evaluating news sources, confirming facts, and distinguishing between trustworthy and dubious information helps build a society resistant to manipulative stories. Introducing media literacy initiatives in educational settings and communities empowers people to make better-informed choices, decreasing vulnerability to propaganda. Additionally, backing organizations dedicated to fact-checking bolsters our collective capacity to spot and challenge falsehoods, maintaining healthy public dialogue.

Remaining alert to misinformation and propaganda is crucial for protecting democratic principles and personal freedom. As highlighted by the NATIONAL ENDOWMENT FOR DEMOCRACY (2018), disinformation is a complex threat that erodes confidence in the media and institutions, stokes social unrest, and obstructs constructive conversation. Cultivating a society that prioritizes evidence, pursues truth, and values diverse perspectives is critical in countering authoritarians' efforts to monopolize information.

To nurture such a society, several steps are helpful. Boosting digital know-how for all ages enables easier identification of disinformation. Facilitating open conversations about current issues within families, educational institutions, and communities sharpens critical thinking and lessens the impact of skewed narratives. Advocating for transparent and accountable governance and media operations builds trust among the public and fights the spread of inaccuracies.

At this point, it's clear that tackling authoritarianism goes beyond just a political challenge—it's also a socio-cultural one that requires everyone to come together. It's absolutely imperative to boost democracy's resilience by encouraging education, critical thinking, and an active participation from the public. Whether you're a government official, policymaker, activist, researcher, or simply someone who cares, the goal is to cultivate a society that remains alert to the signs of authoritarianism and defends the rights and freedoms of everyone.

Chapter 2

The Threat to Civil Liberties

Authoritarian regimes often use various tactics to limit civil liberties and individual freedoms, creating a complex issue that presents itself in many ways. These methods include stifling free speech, excessive surveillance, twisting the legal system to their advantage, and controlling what information the public can access. Such actions restrict people's rights and pose a very serious threat to democracy's very foundations.

The problem goes beyond just the direct victims of authoritarianism. The consequences of silencing voices, invading privacy, corrupting the course of justice, and limiting information flow affect our entire society. They lead to a context where new ideas struggle to emerge, faith in public institutions dwindles, and governance suffers due to a lack of scrutiny. Therefore, the suppression of civil liberties under authoritarian regimes is not only an attack on individual rights but also a critical obstacle to the health and future of democratic systems around the globe.

Suppressing Voices: The Attack on Free Speech

At its core, figuring out how authoritarian regimes maintain control reveals a harsh truth: they often suppress free speech and dissent. This strategy goes beyond just quieting opposition; it aims to weaken the very pillars of democracy and personal freedom by promoting only the perspective approved by those in power. By looking into actual cases, we see the deep freeze this suppression puts on society. It not only affects the brave souls who stand up to speak but also hampers innovation, spreads fear, and erodes trust in public institutions.

One often-missed piece of the puzzle in discussions about authoritarianism is spotting the early warnings of government overreach when it comes to silencing different views. Catching these early warnings is key to stopping the slide towards authoritarianism and pushing back against it. Warning signs like the slow choking off of media freedom, random arrests of activists, and laws meant to quiet opposition should catch our attention. To counter these moves effectively, it's important for individuals and communities to be alert and to encourage society to push back against these incursions on freedom.

Digging deeper into the significance of free speech in a democracy adds more understanding. Free speech is not just another right; it is the foundation that democracy is built upon. It allows for the sharing of ideas, sparks innovation, and helps solve conflicts peacefully by letting people express their concerns openly. When this fundamental right is compromised, authoritarian governments do more than limit personal freedom—they also lower governance quality by shielding themselves from critique and accountability.

Inspiring people to stand up for the right to express diverse viewpoints without fear is very important. It involves acknowledging the immense value of these freedoms and understanding how to safeguard them. This includes advocating for strong legal protections for free speech, backing international human rights initiatives, and utilizing technology to overcome censorship. Equally important is fostering resilience and solidarity among those who uphold democratic principles in the face of challenges and repression.

In today's world, there is an ongoing battle between those who value democratic principles and those who seek to impose authoritarian rule. Organizations such as Freedom House have shed light on a concerning trend: the erosion of democratic freedoms worldwide. This is not just a localized issue; it has far-reaching implications for democracy on a global scale. Authoritarian regimes are becoming increasingly emboldened in their attempts to silence dissent and quash opposition. The consequences of their actions are not limited to their own citizens; they threaten the very foundation of democracy across the entire world.

In the face of these challenges, it is imperative that democratic nations come together in unity and solidarity. Staying vigilant and aware of the threats posed by authoritarianism is key to protecting the fundamental freedoms that so many have fought and sacrificed their lives to secure. By standing together and offering unyielding support to those who are courageously defending their rights against oppressive regimes, democratic nations can send a powerful message: that the principles of freedom, equality, and human rights are non-negotiable.

To address the growing threat of authoritarianism, democratic nations must prioritize cooperation and collaboration. By sharing knowledge, resources, and strategies, they can collectively build a stronger defense against the erosion of democratic values. This may involve diplomatic efforts, economic sanctions, or other measures aimed at holding authoritarian regimes accountable for their actions. By working together, democratic nations can create a formidable front against those who seek to undermine the principles of freedom and democracy.

At the heart of the struggle against authoritarianism lies a commitment to upholding the core values of democracy. These values include the protection of individual rights, the rule of law, and the accountability of those in power to the people they serve. Democratic nations must lead by example, demonstrating their unwavering dedication to these principles both at home and on the global stage. By promoting transparency, accountability, and respect for human rights, they can inspire others to follow suit and contribute to a more just and equitable world.

One of the most effective ways to combat authoritarianism is to support civil society organizations and grassroots activism. These groups play a vital role in advocating for human rights, social justice, and democratic principles. By providing them with resources, funding, and moral support, democratic nations can help amplify their voices and increase their impact. Supporting courageous activists and defenders of freedom sends a powerful message that the world is watching and standing in solidarity with those on the front lines of the struggle for democracy.

The fight against authoritarianism is not just a battle for the present; it is a fight for the future of democracy itself. By working together, staying vigilant, and supporting those who are are risking their lives for freedom, democratic nations can shape a more inclusive, just, and democratic world for generations to come. The challenges may be great, but the resolve of those who believe in freedom and human rights is even greater. As long as democratic nations stand together and remain steadfast in their commitment to upholding democratic values, the beacon of democracy will continue to shine bright, offering hope to all who seek a better, more just world.

Facing these challenges head-on, it's vital for both individuals and societies to learn from history and the experiences of others in similar predicaments. Gaining insights from those who have stood up to tyranny can offer both motivation and actionable advice. This includes getting to grips with the methods used by dictators and identifying effective ways civil societies can respond, such as using international law, fostering safe environments for open dialogue, and forming global alliances to pressure oppressive governments.

Eroding Privacy: Surveillance under Authoritarian Regimes

To grasp how authoritarian governments use surveillance to keep tabs on people, it's important to understand the subtle ways this invades our privacy and affects our freedom. Knowing about the different surveillance tactics out there is key because it gives everyone the tools to spot when they're being watched a little too closely. In today's digital age, where every click and location can be tracked, being alert to how governments might be monitoring us is more important than ever. This awareness isn't just for keeping our personal information safe; it also helps build a resistance against aggressive monitoring and tracking.

Moving forward, it's vital to think about how far governments should go in the name of safety without stepping over the line into our personal space. Leaders of authoritative states often claim they're keeping an eye on everyone for the greater good, to protect the nation. But this shouldn't mean forgetting about everyone's right to have a private life.

Democracies stand strong on the belief that people should know what's going on, especially with something as invasive as surveillance. Pushing for laws and checks to make sure surveillance technologies are used fairly means that we're all playing a part in keeping our freedoms intact.

Privacy matters because it's at the heart of what it means to be free. Living with the constant feeling that 'Big Brother' is always watching shrinks not just our personal space but also affects how freely we make decisions. Picture yourself always under surveillance, every chat, every online search, scrutinized. This can dampen creativity, silence constructive criticism, and weaken trust among people. The stress of being under a watchful eye all the time may cause people to hold back their true feelings or avoid certain actions due to fear of negative consequences.

In a world where surveillance is prevalent, protecting our privacy is essential. One way to do this is by utilizing technology that safeguards our conversations from prying eyes. Secure messaging apps and encrypted emails can help ensure that your discussions remain private and shielded from unwanted intrusion. By taking control of how you communicate, you are actively asserting your right to privacy and autonomy.

Another vital aspect of resisting surveillance is spreading awareness about privacy practices. By sharing information on how to maintain anonymity online, such as using VPNs and avoiding sharing sensitive data on social media, you can empower others to protect themselves. Education is a powerful tool in the fight against intrusive surveillance, as it equips individuals with the knowledge needed to navigate the digital landscape securely.

Supporting legislative changes that limit the scope of surveillance is a vital step in safeguarding personal privacy. By advocating for laws that protect individual rights and restrict unfettered surveillance, we can contribute to creating a legal framework that respects privacy boundaries. Engaging in discussions about privacy laws and supporting policymakers who prioritize data protection can have a significant impact on curbing excessive surveillance practices.

While individual actions are important, collective efforts serve as a formidable defense against intrusive surveillance. Joining forces with like-minded individuals and organizations to advocate for privacy rights can amplify the impact of our resistance. By participating in movements that promote digital freedom and privacy rights, we contribute to creating a more secure and privacy-conscious society.

Every action we take, no matter how seemingly insignificant, contributes to a broader resistance against totalitarian control and unwarranted intrusion into our personal lives. By coming together as a community dedicated to safeguarding privacy, we create a unified front against surveillance practices that threaten our fundamental rights. United in purpose and determination, we can pave the way for a more privacy-respecting future for all.

Thinking critically about balancing safety measures with personal rights goes beyond theory; it's essential for keeping democracies alive. The belief here is that personal freedom and national security aren't opposing goals but can coexist harmoniously. By talking openly, pushing for legal safeguards, and supporting privacy-friendly policies, people have the power to encourage a fair and acceptable balance. Such discussions are key to preventing security concerns from being used as an all-purpose excuse for excessive spying.

The Importance of Open and Accountable Surveillance Procedures

One key aspect of ensuring that surveillance practices are carried out responsibly is the establishment of clear and strict rules. These rules are vitally important as they help in regulating surveillance activities and safeguarding the rights of individuals. For instance, one important rule could be requiring any surveillance operation to obtain approval from a court before it is carried out. This step ensures that there is oversight and accountability in the surveillance process.

To enhance accountability and transparency in surveillance practices, it is essential to have mechanisms for regular oversight. This can involve periodic reviews of surveillance activities by designated authorities. By conducting regular checks and evaluations, it becomes possible to identify any potential misuse of surveillance technologies and address any compliance issues promptly.

Creating bodies with the authority to monitor and enforce compliance with surveillance rules is another critical step in ensuring accountability. These oversight bodies play an important role in ensuring that surveillance practices adhere to established guidelines and do not infringe on individuals' privacy rights. By empowering such bodies, it becomes possible to hold those engaging in surveillance accountable for their actions.

By instituting and adhering to strict controls on surveillance practices, societies can reap significant benefits. Responsible surveillance not only protects individual privacy and rights but also contributes to the overall well-being of the community. When surveillance technologies are used ethically and transparently, they can serve the interests of the public by enhancing security, preventing crimes, and ensuring the effective functioning of law enforcement agencies.

Implementing robust surveillance regulations is essential in guarding against the concentration of power in authoritarian governments. By placing limits on surveillance activities and ensuring checks and balances are in place, it becomes more challenging for governments to abuse surveillance technologies for their own political gain. This, in turn, helps in preserving democratic principles and safeguarding individual freedoms within a society.

Legal Systems as Tools of Oppression

Authoritarian governments are using legal systems to limit personal freedoms, which poses a serious threat to democracy worldwide. These governments silence critics to weaken democratic values. This is not just a theoretical issue; it affects fairness and justice globally. Laws about sedition and terrorism are often misused to stop dissent, branding activism and peaceful protests as hostile, or even as terrorism. This not only limits different political views but also makes people afraid to support democracy.

To push back against these disturbing patterns, it's essential to spread awareness by educating yourself and others on how laws can be twisted to quash free speech. Support organizations that keep an eye on legal fairness and power abuses, and promote changes locally or nationally to safeguard the freedom to disagree without fear of wrongful persecution.

When legal safeguards that protect freedom of speech and assembly are diluted, it does more than just silence critics. It also weakens the foundation of democratic participation. By imposing restrictions on speaking out and gathering, individuals' ability to have a say in policymaking diminishes. This limitation not only dampens their voices but also serves as a warning sign of declining democratic vitality, which could potentially open the door to tyranny.

The implications of these restrictions are not confined to the realm of theory; they have tangible impacts on the lives of individuals and on society as a whole. When people are unable to freely express their opinions or assemble to peacefully protest or advocate for change, the democratic process suffers. It creates a stifling atmosphere where dissent is suppressed, hindering the exchange of diverse viewpoints essential for a healthy democratic society.

The erosion of legal safeguards that protect expression and engagement reverberates throughout society, touching various aspects of public life. When individuals feel constrained in voicing their opinions or organizing for causes they believe in, the vibrancy of public discourse fades. This, in turn, hampers the ability of a society to address challenges collectively and innovate through the exchange of ideas and perspectives.

A decline in legal protections for freedom of expression and assembly poses a direct threat to democratic principles. These safeguards are fundamental pillars that uphold the rights of individuals to participate in the democratic process and hold those in power accountable. Diluting these protections jeopardizes the checks and balances necessary for a functioning democracy and creates a power imbalance that undermines the voice of the people.

However, acknowledging these issues is only the start. The critical role of an independent judiciary in maintaining democracy's balance cannot be emphasized enough. It serves as a defense against other government branches' overreach, safeguarding individual rights in the pursuit of power. Supporting judicial independence doesn't require intricate legal knowledge but a dedication to the principles of justice and human rights. Advocating for merit-based judicial appointments, resisting political pressures, and fostering judicial transparency are key steps in this direction.

In facing these challenges, empowering people to legally challenge unfair laws shines a hopeful light. Taking legal action against oppressive legislation offers a direct form of resistance and establishes precedents that bolster legal defenses for everyone. Nevertheless, pursuing this avenue needs resources, skilled expertise, and broad support. Get to know the legal system and the rights it provides against government overreach. Help or join groups providing legal assistance to those fighting unjust laws. Foster conversations and partnerships between legal professionals, activists, and communities to strongly defend civil rights.

Drawing inspiration from Freedom House's 2022 report, we observe the troubling spread of authoritarian rule and its systematic erosion of democratic norms and institutions, including those ensuring individual freedoms. These developments highlight that defending the rule of law goes beyond legal duties; it's a moral obligation critical for preserving democracy. To counteract authoritarian tendencies, recognizing these tactics and actively working to bolster democratic resilience are imperative steps.

Censorship and Control: Limiting Access to Information

To understand the impacts of censorship, start by acknowledging how it directly threatens our individual freedom and the well-being of society as a whole. Censorship acts like a barrier to the free flow of ideas and conversations that are the backbone of any thriving democracy. By blocking different viewpoints and limiting open discussions, it undermines what's known as the 'marketplace of ideas.' This is a metaphorical space where different concepts clash and the best ones emerge victorious based on their strength and appeal, not because they're the only options available. Such competition is vital for the growth of society's norms and values and for individuals' intellectual development, allowing us to think critically, ask questions, and grow in our understanding of the world.

Furthermore, when information is manipulated, it plays right into the agenda of those wanting to steer public opinion their way. At this juncture, it becomes vital to highlight the connection between being savvy about media and thinking critically—a skill set that's becoming increasingly important. In today's world, bombarded by propaganda and misinformation, the ability to sift through the noise and identify trustworthy content is key. Promoting media literacy, therefore, is not just beneficial but essential. It encourages us to approach various sources with a critical eye, spot biases, and separate credible information from rumors or falsehoods, thereby contributing significantly to a well-informed and democratic society.

Reflecting further on censorship's role in shaping public narratives reveals its extensive reach. When voices are silenced, society loses out on the rich tapestry of diverse experiences and insights. By controlling what realities or perspectives people can access, censorship skews our collective understanding, entrenching existing power imbalances and silencing alternative views. These tactics risk distorting not just current events but history itself, paving the path for historical revisionism and the erasure of inconvenient truths.

Fostering a culture of defending the free flow of information stands out as an effective way to counteract censorship and misinformation. This involves both personal responsibility and collaborative efforts. Individuals are encouraged to speak up for transparency and hold legacy media and governments accountable, while collectively, there's a need for unity in battling misleading narratives. This collective effort can manifest in numerous ways, ranging from supporting independent journalism to advocating for policy changes that protect our right to information.

This proactive stance not only addresses the immediate issues of censorship and propaganda but also fosters a broader cultural shift towards valuing open dialogue. A society enriched by a diversity of viewpoints is better equipped to face its challenges and innovate, creating an environment where progress is possible.

Ensuring that everyone has access to unfiltered information is crucial for developing an informed citizenry capable of meaningful participation in democracy. As pointed out by UNESCO, social media bypass traditional gatekeeping, allowing ideas, including populism, to spread more freely. This highlights the importance of maintaining direct access to information so people can form their own opinions based on a full understanding of the facts, rather than through manipulated narratives. In the digital age, where the line between fact and opinion is increasingly blurred, protecting this access is more important than ever.

The duty falls on us as individuals, communities, and entire nations to acknowledge, challenge, and overturn the authoritarian tactics that threaten our rights. The ripple effects of choosing inaction or indifference reach well beyond the erosion of our personal freedoms—they put at risk the foundation of global democratic principles and the prospect for future generations to experience open, equitable societies.

Chapter 3

The Role of Technology in Authoritarianism

We live in times marked by rapid technological growth, yet this progress casts a long shadow when it comes to the power it gives governments to tighten their control over societies. Tools for surveillance and various online platforms can serve two masters: they can open up incredible avenues for oversight and influence by state powers, blurring the line between protection and intrusion. This situation raises critical ethical concerns, making us rethink our understanding of privacy and freedom. It's becoming increasingly clear that technology can sneak into the most intimate aspects of our lives, disguised as measures for safety or effectiveness, prompting us to question how we balance state interests with the rights of individuals.

At the core of this dilemma is how tyrannical governments use technology to cement their authority, transforming what were initially seen as tools for enhancing democracy into instruments of oppression. With surveillance growing more pervasive and social media turning into arenas for contesting narratives, the boundaries between what is public and private begin to fade. This worrying shift not only limits our personal freedoms but also chokes off dissent and shapes public opinion, weakening the pillars of open debate. The unchecked acceleration of these tactics points to a deepening conflict between the advancement of technology and the safeguarding of fundamental human liberties, signifying the pressing need to fully grasp these issues.

Surveillance Technologies: Instruments of Oppression

Surveillance tools like facial recognition and tracking software have given governments with authoritarian leanings the power to watch and pinpoint those who oppose them like never before. This shift in how surveillance is used—a move from general oversight to in-depth monitoring—signals a worrying trend for anyone who values personal freedom over governmental control.

These technologies aren't just sitting in the background; they're actively changing the rules of the game. Knowing that you could be watched at any moment – whether you're walking down the street or just making a phone call – creates a culture of fear. It's as though an unseen eye is always there, pushing people toward silence out of fear rather than through direct intimidation. A terrifying vision of an Orwellian Dystopian future comes to mind.

However, it's not a hopeless situation. Becoming aware of these surveillance tactics opens up ways to fight back. By educating ourselves on digital privacy tools like encryption and secure networks, we can keep our conversations private. Pushing for clear rules about when and how surveillance tech can be used adds a layer of protection. And by choosing technology that values our privacy, we help build a demand for more ethical options.

This newfound knowledge not only empowers us but also lights a fire under advocacy efforts. Realizing just how intrusive these technologies can be highlights the urgent need for laws that respect our privacy while keeping us safe. It's a wakeup call for everyone to support regulations that value and protect our personal space in this digital era, echoing the concerns raised by Parsons in 2019 about the dangers of unchecked surveillance capitalism.

Looking back at history shows us the dark paths surveillance can lead us down when left unchecked. These lessons from the past are crucial; they show us the slippery slope from safety measures to mechanisms of control. They remind us to stay alert and push for a collective agreement on the limits of watching and recording.

At its core, the debate around surveillance asks us what kind of future we want. Are we okay with living in a world where our every step could be tracked, or do we fight for a place where we can be free from constant observation? This isn't an easy question, but it's essential we ask it. Raising awareness and standing up for privacy rights are no longer optional; they're imperative if we hope to maintain our dignity in a world wrapped in surveillance.

Moving forward means having real conversations and taking action. It's about bringing together different voices— government representatives, activists, and everyday people— to craft solutions that respect both security and personal freedom. Demanding clear rules and accountability for how surveillance tech is used is vital. At the same time, backing innovations that protect our privacy gives us alternatives that don't make us choose between being safe and being free.

Facial Recognition Technology

Facial recognition technology is a tool used in some countries like China and the UK. This technology involves scanning people's faces to identify them. It's like when you take a selfie and your phone recognizes your face to unlock it. In these countries, they use this technology aggressively. Imagine walking down the street and a camera can tell who you are just by looking at your face.

When you stand in front of a camera, the camera does something interesting. It analyzes your face very carefully, like when you look at pictures on your phone. But the camera is much faster and more sophisticated than human eyes. It takes just a quick moment to scan your face.

The surveillance cameras used by governments are all connected to enormous databases that stores a vast collection of photos and data of billions private citizens, like a digital picture album. It scans your face and compares it to all of the other faces in this extensive collection. If it finds a similar face in this archive, it can confidently declare a positive match.

Once the facial recognition software identifies a matching face in its extensive database, it can then access all the data that the government has collected about you to positively determine your identity. In just a matter of seconds, these intrusive technologies enable governments to gather detailed information about individuals without their consent. Surveillance cameras equipped with this technology in countries like China and the UK have been installed though out many major cities to identify private citizens and ascertain their identities.

Facial recognition technology can violate people's privacy, akin to someone snooping through your personal diary without your permission. Individuals should have the authority to decide who can access their confidential information and when. The discomfort of being monitored unknowingly can be unsettling. In certain regions, governments heavily rely on this technology, leading to a constant sensation of being under observation in the most routine moments.

Mass surveillance involves the monitoring of a specific area through numerous cameras, creating a pervasive network of surveillance. This approach is utilized in countries such as

China and the United Kingdom, where individuals may be subject to continuous observation without their awareness.

Imagine going to the park and knowing there are cameras seeing everything you do. It's like having a secret audience watch your every move. In these countries, mass surveillance is a big part of life. It's like a giant net catching everything that happens. This constant surveillance can make people feel like they can't relax and be themselves.

When governments implement mass surveillance, it grants them control over people's actions. It's akin to constantly being monitored by an authoritative figure dictating your every move. In nations with widespread surveillance, individuals may sense a restriction on their liberty. This method of control is commonly employed by oppressive regimes and bears a striking resemblance to the fictional dystopian society portrayed in George Orwell's novel, 1984.

In some countries, the use of facial recognition technology and mass surveillance creates a reality that mirrors a science fiction movie. We now exist in a world where our actions are never truly private, blurring the line between reality and fiction when we uncover how these technologies operate. The once distant future depicted in fictional novels is now unfolding right before our eyes.

Social Media: A Battlefield for Propaganda

To understand how technology supports authoritarian rule, we need to explore how social media and the internet can be used against us to spread false narratives. The manipulation of online spaces to share lies, influence public opinion, and maintain authoritarian power is concerning. This approach not only challenges democratic values but also creates a fake world that supports authoritarian goals. In this made-up reality, the truth can be twisted and reshaped.

Technology's role has dramatically changed from being seen as a beacon of freedom to becoming a mechanism of control. Once celebrated as tools for spreading democracy, social media platforms are now being used by authoritarian governments to strengthen their hold on power. This flip highlights the complicated dynamics between tech progress and political control, prompting us to rethink our views on digital liberties.

Identifying what's true versus state-crafted propaganda poses a major challenge. Authoritarian governments have become adept at dressing up their propaganda as legitimate news, taking advantage of the thin line between fact and fiction online. They exploit bots and trolls to amplify their misinformation, making it harder to separate truth from lies. Here, the importance of critical media literacy shines through. Teaching people how to critically analyze online content arms them with the ability to sift through digital deception.

To enhance your digital literacy, consider checking information from several trusted sources before believing it. Learn about common online manipulation tactics, such as emotional triggers and phony experts. Research a variety of perspectives to break free from echo chambers that confirm existing prejudices.

Understanding the impact of social media on how we perceive the world helps us grasp its influence on societal values and opinions. It goes beyond recognizing the prevalence of propaganda and includes understanding how content algorithms trap users in ideological bubbles. This division not only fragments public discourse but also amplifies the narratives crafted by authoritarian governments, complicating efforts to establish a consensus on factual truths.

Moreover, learning to recognize authenticity amidst propaganda does more than sharpen individual skills—it acts as a communal shield. It fortifies society against attacks on democratic principles and free expression. When people can spot and reject authoritarian messages, they help create a collective safeguard that protects open dialogue and democracy. This united resilience is key to defending democratic ideals and keeping the marketplace of ideas lively and varied.

Critical media literacy plays a vital role in resisting digital authoritarianism. It helps citizens analyze information critically and encourages skepticism towards attempts to influence public conversations. Therefore, advancing media literacy is not just about education but a necessary step in safeguarding democracy against authoritarian tactics.

As authoritarian regimes refine their digital strategies to cling to power, democratic societies must innovate in educating their citizens. The future depends on unwavering dedication to teaching and raising awareness, establishing defenses based on critical thinking about the media we consume.

Data Harvesting: The Threat to Individual Autonomy

Understanding the dangers of data harvesting is essential in this era of rapid digital transformation. As we dive into the age of tech advances, it's clear that our personal freedom hangs in the balance. The way authoritarian regimes gather data isn't just about losing privacy; it's a means to pinpoint and suppress freedom without individuals' consent. Imagine a reality where your every online action, each site you browse, and even how you physically move could be analyzed and used to control you, all without your consent.

In this modern age, there exists a significant threat to both our privacy and our ability to determine our own path. This threat comes from the collection of information by powerful entities. When governments or corporations amass large amounts of data about individuals, they gain unprecedented abilities to observe and potentially manipulate our behaviors and beliefs. It's like having someone constantly looking over our shoulders, knowing our every move and thought. This might seem surreal, but various studies have shown that technologies like virtual reality can accurately identify individuals based on their movements. This development raises valid concerns about the erosion of our privacy and the rise of unrestricted surveillance.

Imagine a world where every step we take is monitored, every action noted, and every decision observed. This is the reality that emerges when vast amounts of personal data are collected and analyzed. Governments and businesses, armed with sophisticated technology, can track individuals with alarming precision. This level of surveillance raises red flags about the potential loss of our personal space and the constant scrutiny we might unknowingly come under.

Not only does the collection of data pose a threat to our privacy, but it also opens doors for external influences to shape our thoughts and actions. When powerful entities have access to comprehensive information about us, they can tailor their messages and interventions to manipulate our decisions. It's like being in a game where the rules are set by someone else who knows your every move. The fear of being subtly nudged or coerced into certain behaviors is real in a world where data collection is rampant.

The pervasive nature of data collection means that our lives become an open book, easily readable by those in positions of authority. Whether it's a government agency or a large corporation, the capacity to monitor individuals at such a granular level raises serious concerns about the unchecked power this information provides. The constant surveillance that comes with data collection creates a dynamic where our every action is subject to scrutiny, potentially leading to a society where personal autonomy is at risk.

As technology advances and data collection methods become more sophisticated, the concerns surrounding privacy and self-determination continue to grow. The ability to track individuals through virtual reality or other advanced means amplifies the risks of unauthorized surveillance and manipulation. In a world where personal data is constantly harvested and analyzed, the line between individual freedom and external control becomes increasingly blurred. This trend raises important questions about the balance between technological progress and the protection of fundamental human rights.

The increasing amount of power and control that these technologies give governments and corporations is extremely dangerous to our autonomy. The powerful abilities of governments and businesses to monitor and influence individuals based on collected data underscore the need for robust safeguards to protect personal freedoms. In a society where surveillance has become pervasive, it is crucial to maintain a critical stance on the impact of data collection practices on our rights and liberties. As we navigate this landscape of evolving technologies and increasing data collection, awareness of the risks and a proactive approach to safeguarding privacy are essential to preserving our individuality and self-determination.

But there's power in awareness. Knowing how and why our data is being exploited allows us to start defending ourselves. To better protect your data privacy, think carefully about what permissions you give to apps and services, allowing only what really needs access. Frequently check and adjust your online accounts' privacy settings, and support platforms that make user privacy a priority.

Asking tech companies for transparency isn't just about making them responsible; it's about taking back our right to understand how our data is utilized. Only by working together and demanding higher standards can we hope to prompt a shift towards more ethical handling of our private data.

Calling for stronger laws to protect our data is key to keeping our rights safe in the digital world. Laws like the GDPR in the European Union are examples for the world, giving people more control over their personal data. However, the journey towards solid data protection laws that truly grasp today's tech is still going. It's important to get policymakers to see and tackle these issues to keep our privacy rights intact in an ever-growing digital society.

Looking into the fallout of uncontrolled data gathering goes beyond just worrying about privacy; it underlines how important it is for us to be aware and active about digital privacy. In times when data is as valuable as money, knowing its worth and the dangers of its mishandling is vital. Awareness initiatives, educational efforts, and being part of digital rights groups are fundamental in building a community that cherishes and defends digital privacy.

Although it seems daunting, keeping our data safe is vital for maintaining our freedom in the digital realm. It takes a united effort from everyone—users, tech firms, lawmakers, and activists—to make sure technological progress doesn't crush our basic rights. As technology pushes forward rapidly, our strategies for privacy defense and advocacy must also evolve. Remember, at the core of digital progress should always be a commitment to respect human dignity and freedom.

AI and Algorithms: Manipulating Public Opinion

The rapid growth of artificial intelligence (AI) and how algorithms affect public opinion are starting an important discussion on the need for people to understand media better and have clear rules for algorithms. AI's ability to personalize what we see on the internet impacts how we view the world and changes our thoughts on different subjects like governance. It's not just about choosing which articles or posts show up in our social media; it's about influencing what society thinks by promoting certain viewpoints over others. AI might keep us in echo chambers where we only hear the same ideas, not new ones, making it tough to see the whole picture.

To counter these risks, it's key that we all get a good grasp on how these algorithms decide what content to show us. Knowing more about this helps everyone make better judgments about the news and stories we find online. It's important to encourage people to interact with a wide array of digital content critically and seek out varied sources of information. This approach helps break down the walls of those echo chambers.

It's also vital to recognize how AI algorithms can reinforce biases. By only showing us views we already agree with, they limit our exposure to different ideas and fuel misinformation. This situation makes it hard to have open discussions, which are the backbone of democracy. Encouraging conversations across different viewpoints is essential.

Furthermore, understanding the wider societal effects of algorithm control highlights the necessity of demanding more openness and responsibility from those developing these technologies. This action not only uncovers how algorithms work but also allows communities to push for AI to meet ethical standards. We have to back laws and policies that make companies reveal how their algorithms function, and we must call for independent checks of algorithms to ensure they're fair and do not violate our rights or freedoms.

Organizations like Freedom House emphasize the importance of strong rules to protect human rights online, pointing out how authoritarian regimes use AI to tighten their grip and silence opposition. This reality makes it vital to remain alert and take proactive steps to maintain the core values of democracy and free speech.

There's a complex relationship between technology, governance, and human rights requiring a comprehensive response. Individuals must become savvy about the digital world, and policymakers need to create laws that encourage innovation while safeguarding essential liberties. Working together, different sectors can lead us to an era where technology truly benefits society, supporting rather than eroding democratic values.

Although technology offers the potential to boost democratic participation, its exploitation by authoritarian governments poses a significant threat to the liberties and privacy of individuals. This issue is especially pertinent for government officials, policy makers, activists, academics in social sciences, and anyone concerned about preserving civil liberties in the face of growing authoritarianism.

The unchecked dominion of technology highlights a critical worry for the wellbeing of democracies worldwide. As we grapple with these issues, it's clear that creating a culture of critical engagement with digital media, alongside strong legal protections and ethical advancement in technology, is of the upmost importance.

Chapter 4

The Erosion of Privacy in the Digital Age

In today's digital-first environment, privacy has shifted from a basic entitlement to a luxury that feels increasingly out of reach. The internet's broad sweep, enhanced by advanced data-gathering technologies, means our personal information doesn't just belong to us anymore. It's now part of a much larger digital realm, open to numerous groups for reasons we might not fully understand. This shift has sparked an intense debate about the safety of our most personal details in an era dominated by digital existence.

This problem is about how data is collected, processed, and shared on the internet. People often add to their online profiles without knowing, through every click, search, and interaction online. This has led to a shady business in personal information, turning what people like, do, and when they do it, into things that can be sold. These actions not only make it hard to keep our private lives private but also show how our information could be misused, highlighting a lack of trust between consumers and the big digital companies. Also, since we have little control over our online presence, this shows a significant difference in power, making us vulnerable to hidden dangers.

Corporate Data Collection: A Threat to Personal Privacy

The digital world is incredibly large, and corporate data collection practices are at the center of it, affecting nearly every online activity. This situation has a big impact on our privacy and calls for a careful discussion. Essentially, companies profile users extensively, which could lead to privacy violations and increased surveillance. Imagine a scenario where each of your online activities, like clicks and views, is tracked, often without you knowing or agreeing to it. This results in a digital record that is as unique as your fingerprints.

Many companies say they gather this data to offer tailored services and products, which supposedly improves our online experiences. Sounds good, right? However, this raises concerns about the fine line between helpful customization and unwanted snooping. Our personal information becomes a product in itself, bought and sold in the marketplace. This situation affects more than just the ads you see; it can influence your credit rating and even your job opportunities. The lack of transparency about how and why our data is used leaves many of us feeling exposed and without control.

When we take a closer look at how data moves between different companies, things start to get more complicated. Imagine you sign up for a new app or website, and you agree to their terms and conditions. Your data doesn't just stay with that one company; it can travel to many other companies without you even realizing it. These companies are connected in a web, like a spider's web, with threads reaching everywhere, carrying bits and pieces of information about you. This can be risky because your data could end up in the wrong hands without you knowing it.

As your information spreads through these interconnected companies, it becomes harder to know who exactly has access to it. Think of it like playing a game of "pass the parcel" at a party, where the parcel is your data. You give it to one person, who gives it to another, and so on. Each hand it passes through is another opportunity for your data to be misused or leaked. It's like a secret that gets shared among friends but might accidentally slip out to someone you don't want knowing it.

With your data floating around in this vast network of interconnected companies, your privacy is at stake. You might be diligent about protecting your information with the companies you directly deal with, but what about the ones they share it with? It's like trying to guard a treasure in a maze where the walls keep shifting, and you can never be sure who's lurking around the next corner. This uncertainty can make you feel exposed and vulnerable in the digital world.

This intricate network of data sharing creates a persistent worry for individuals about their digital security. It's like having a cloud hanging over your head, always reminding you that your personal information is out there, beyond your control. Every time you agree to a new service or disclose your details online, you add another layer to this complex web, increasing the chances of a data breach or misuse. It's a bit like walking on a tightrope, trying to maintain balance amidst the constant flow of information around you.

In this evolving landscape of data sharing, awareness is key. Understanding how your information moves through these networks can empower you to make informed choices about what you share and with whom. It's like being the captain of your own ship, navigating through choppy waters with a map in hand. By educating yourself about data privacy and taking active steps to protect your information, you can reduce the risks associated with being part of this expansive data-sharing ecosystem.

Many companies often mishandle users' private data for profit-driven motives. Facebook, now known as META, stands out as a prime example of exploiting data for financial gain. The company has an extensive track record of being implicated in numerous user data breaches and leaks over the years.

- In 2018, Facebook announced a security breach that exposed the accounts of 50 million users.
- In 2019, a third-party app exposed 540 million records, including Facebook IDs, comments, likes, and reaction data.

- In 2019, another data scrape exposed 419 million Facebook user records, including hundreds of millions of phone numbers, names, and Facebook IDs.
- In 2021, a massive data breach exposed the personal information of half a billion Facebook users, including phone numbers and biographical information.

It's difficult to pinpoint the exact number of times Facebook has mishandled user data. There could be additional incidents undisclosed to the public. Nonetheless, these instances reveal Facebook's involvement in numerous significant data breaches and leaks throughout the years.

Data harvesting across networks of companies presents a dynamic and intricate web of challenges for individuals concerned about their privacy and security. The interconnected nature of these data flows highlights the importance of staying vigilant and informed in an increasingly digital world. By recognizing the complex landscape of data harvesting and taking proactive measures to safeguard personal information, individuals can navigate this web of connections with greater confidence and control.

But here's a bit of good news: you can take steps to safeguard your privacy. Being mindful about what personal information you share online is a great starting point. Simple actions like tweaking your social media settings, using strong passwords, and staying alert to phishing scams can make a big difference in reducing your online presence. Additionally, pushing for stronger laws to protect our data is vital. Privacy should be seen as a basic right, not a luxury or something to be traded.

Taking steps to protect your data involves forming a routine of reading through the privacy policies of websites and apps, understanding the specifics of the information they gather and the reasons behind it. Advocating for policy adjustments to strengthen consumer privacy, urging companies to handle our data with care. These steps go beyond personal defense; they signify a call for a shift in how corporations manage our data.

The Impact of Government Surveillance on Privacy Rights

In today's digital world, the balance between privacy and government surveillance is hotly debated. The rise of advanced surveillance technologies has presented a significant challenge to personal freedom and autonomy. These technologies are often introduced under the guise of national security, but they bring about serious privacy concerns.

Surveillance programs have become a significant concern due to their tendency to gather extensive amounts of information from ordinary individuals. The data collected often includes highly personal details that are unrelated to any security threats. This practice not only violates individuals' privacy but also exposes them to the potential misuse or exploitation of their information. Organizations like the American Civil Liberties Union (ACLU) emphasize that the unwarranted collection of data represents a violation of privacy rights that are fundamental to every citizen.

The indiscriminate collection of data by surveillance programs poses a direct threat to personal privacy. When such programs amass vast quantities of information, they create opportunities for unauthorized access and misuse. This indiscriminate data collection undermines the foundation of privacy rights that individuals should inherently possess. The potential for authorities to access and utilize personal information without valid justification raises concerns about the misuse and abuse of such data.

The handling of personal data without a legitimate reason poses ethical and legal challenges. Surveillance programs that collect data without proper justification violate individuals' rights and principles of privacy protection. The ACLU's position on data collection emphasizes the ethical aspects of these practices and underscores the importance of safeguarding citizens' privacy rights. The misuse of personal data acquired through surveillance can have significant consequences, leading to breaches of trust and ethical boundaries.

One of the critical issues stemming from surveillance programs is the lack of transparency regarding data security measures. When personal information is collected without clear guidelines or oversight, individuals are left vulnerable to potential breaches and unauthorized access. The absence of transparent data management practices raises concerns about how information is stored, shared, and protected within these programs. As a result, individuals may be unaware of the extent to which their data is being used and the risks associated with its storage and dissemination.

The enduring nature of data collected by surveillance programs raises concerns about its long-term implications. Once personal information is in the hands of authorities, it can be stored indefinitely, creating a perpetual risk of exposure and exploitation. The lack of defined data retention policies and oversight mechanisms further exacerbates the potential for long-term privacy threats. Individuals may find themselves subject to ongoing monitoring and data retention without their explicit consent or awareness.

Surveillance programs operate under ambiguous policies that can change without public knowledge or consent. The lack of transparency in how data is managed and shared within these programs contributes to a broader lack of accountability. Individuals may not be adequately informed about the rules governing their data, leading to potential violations of their privacy rights. The shifting nature of data management policies within surveillance programs underscores the importance of establishing clear guidelines and increasing accountability measures to safeguard personal information.

The unchecked collection of personal data by surveillance programs brings inherent risks, opening the door to potential misuse and exploitation. Authorities having extensive information about individuals without valid reasons can lead to unwarranted surveillance or profiling. The lack of proper oversight and accountability puts individuals at risk of abuse of power and privacy violations. To prevent unauthorized access and exploitation, safeguarding against the misuse of personal data requires robust protections, clear guidelines, and diligent oversight.

The concerns surrounding surveillance programs and their impact on personal privacy highlight the need for greater transparency, accountability, and ethical considerations in data collection practices. Balancing the imperative of security with respect for individual privacy rights is vital to avoid the potential risks associated with unchecked surveillance. Addressing the ethical, legal, and security implications of data collection is essential to protecting individuals' privacy and upholding fundamental rights in the digital age.

The moral questions surrounding government surveillance add another layer of complexity. It's essential to weigh the pros and cons carefully: Do the security benefits of surveillance outweigh the infringement on individual freedoms? We need to thoughtfully examine if these programs are effective in preventing threats and if that effectiveness justifies their invasive nature.

It's also key to fully understand the scope of government surveillance efforts. As surveillance technology advances, staying informed about what these activities involve is very important. Without clear transparency, holding those in power accountable becomes difficult, as does fully comprehending how surveillance affects our daily lives and democracy as a whole.

Individuals can become actively involved and advocate for more accountable surveillance practices by pushing for policies that require government agencies to openly disclose information about their surveillance practices and the actions they take to safeguard our rights. Support changes in legislation that enhance oversight and implement stricter regulations on government utilization of surveillance technology. Maintaining awareness and staying informed about the latest advancements in surveillance technology and legal changes is crucial for a better comprehension of their implications on privacy and civil liberties.

Taking these actions helps us all work together to maintain our privacy rights amid increasing government surveillance. Recognizing the threat surveillance poses to privacy is the first step. Equally important is fighting for better oversight, legal changes, and mechanisms for public accountability to limit surveillance program expansion. Continuous commitment and advocacy are vital for achieving a fair balance between national security needs and our fundamental freedoms.

Ironically, surveillance programs intended to protect national security might undermine the very principles they're supposed to safeguard. This contradiction highlights the importance of critically examining and discussing the place of surveillance in democratic societies. By engaging in this dialogue, backed by facts and a dedication to civil liberties, we can face the challenges of the digital age without sacrificing our core values.

Central Bank Digital Currency (CBDC) - A Threat to Financial Privacy

With the rise of Central Bank Digital Currency (CBDC), there is a disturbing trend that poses a significant threat to our democracy. The central banks are pushing for the widespread adoption of digital currency, aiming to phase out physical currency completely. This shift would place full control of our money in the hands of the Central Bank, stripping away our financial privacy and autonomy. Imagine a world where every financial transaction you make is monitored and controlled by a central authority – this is the reality that CBDCs bring with them.

In Canada, a similar oppressive approach unfolded during the 2022 Freedom Convoy. Prime Minister Justin Trudeau enacted severe measures akin to the tyrannical tactics that might be found in a dictator's playbook, such as freezing the bank accounts of protesters and their supporters to suppress the right to peaceful protest. Consider how if authoritarian regimes worldwide adopted this level of control over lawful citizens exercising their rights. Any form of dissent could be swiftly silenced with the press of a button. This is our potential future if we permit CBDCs to replace physical currency.

The implementation of CBDCs is not just a theoretical concern; China has already rolled out its digital Yuan, showcasing the potential dangers of such a system. In China, the government exercises tight control over the digital currency, going as far as experimenting with the concept of expiration dates on funds. This move aims to restrict individuals from saving and accumulating wealth, ensuring perpetual reliance on the authoritarian regime for financial stability.

The core danger of CBDCs lies in the unyielding control they grant to governments over their citizens' financial lives. By centralizing currency in a digital form, individuals risk becoming entirely dependent on the whims of ruling authorities. The prospect of financial freedom and autonomy fades away, leaving individuals vulnerable to the unchecked power of the state. Once this control is established, regaining personal financial sovereignty becomes a nearly insurmountable challenge.

In the face of CBDCs, the potential ramifications for our democracy are profound. The erosion of financial privacy and independence sets a dangerous precedent, paving the way for increased government interference in personal affairs. As history has shown, the relinquishing of liberty in the realm of finance often leads to broader infringements on individual rights. The implementation of CBDCs represents a pivotal moment in our societal evolution, one that demands careful consideration and proactive safeguarding of our fundamental freedoms.

Ethical Considerations in the Digital Handling of Data

In this day and age, as we navigate through the digital era, we come across various ethical challenges related to how personal information is handled online. Every action we take - be it clicking on a link, swiping on an app, or typing on a keyboard - leads to our data being gathered, saved, and used by different groups. This situation brings up important questions about privacy and the way our information is managed, urging us to pay close attention to these matters more than ever.

The way our personal data is captured and used in the online world introduces ethical questions that can't be ignored. Without solid ethical principles and rules guiding them, there's a real risk that this information could be misused. It's crucial that the development and use of digital technologies are driven by ethics, ensuring they benefit society without violating our rights or freedoms. Striking the right balance between advancing technology and adhering to ethical standards in handling data is key. We must strive for a balanced approach to managing and governing data that places human rights above pure economic gain, showing a true dedication to individual freedom and societal responsibility.

Furthermore, it's important for both individuals and organizations to emphasize the ethical use of data to build a sense of trust and openness within the digital environment. This includes respecting the choices of users, getting proper consent for using their information, and upholding strict security measures to protect data. Trust forms the foundation of any positive interaction between tech providers and their users. By sticking to ethical guidelines, companies can create a trustworthy atmosphere not only preserving user information but also enhancing their own reputations as dependable custodians of data.

Keeping user information safe is important to maintain high ethical standards in managing data. Balancing innovation and ethical technology use is tricky. Regular discussions are needed among lawmakers, tech experts, and the general public to navigate digital ethics. It's important to make ethical choices when creating and using new tech. As we dive deeper into digital innovation, it's increasingly vital to include ethical considerations in technological progress. This ensures that advancements benefit everyone without compromising our core principles and values.

Organizations and individuals alike should make ethical data usage a priority, realizing that careful management of data is essential to maintain trust and integrity online. Companies can show their dedication to ethical data handling by setting clear usage policies that respect the privacy and choices of users and communicating openly with users about the purposes behind data collection, giving them control over their own information.

Understanding the ethical challenges of data use is very important. Embracing responsible conduct is key to advancing data ethics and safeguarding privacy. These concerns go beyond mere regulations; they are fundamental principles that should govern our actions in the digital realm. As we navigate the ever-expansive digital landscape, it is imperative to uphold ethical considerations, ensuring our digital future mirrors the values of respect, integrity, and fairness for all.

Lessons from Case Studies on Privacy Breaches

In today's digital age, every online action we take, from clicking on a link to sharing a post, leaves behind traces that blur the boundaries between our private lives and the public domain. The rising number of cyber incidents serves as a grim reminder of how vulnerable our digital world is. A notable example includes a software flaw that compromised the privacy of 1.2% of ChatGPT Plus users, alongside three separate incidents at Samsung Semiconductor due to employee interactions with ChatGPT, highlighting the complex risks we face (Harvard Business Review, 2023). These instances underscore the critical need for stronger measures to protect our data and ensure our privacy.

Privacy breaches have serious consequences, affecting not just individuals but society as a whole. Those directly affected might experience financial losses and emotional stress while trying to restore their identity and sense of security. These incidents can make people lose trust in online platforms and institutions, which could slow down progress and innovation. This caution in using digital technology highlights the importance of safeguarding personal information proactively.

Taking lessons from previous privacy mishaps is key to strengthening our defenses against new cyber threats. The 2017 Equifax breach affected around 147 million people, resulting in lawsuits, resignations, and a substantial settlement (Kara, 2021), showing what can happen when cybersecurity is not taken seriously. These examples highlight the importance of having strong security protocols, updating systems regularly, and conducting thorough risk assessments to prevent potential threats. By learning from these incidents, businesses and governments can craft more effective strategies to protect data and respond to breaches, adapting to the ever-evolving tactics of cybercriminals.

Raising awareness is crucial, but it's not enough to combat data breaches. We need a culture built on accountability and preventive actions. Guidelines provide a roadmap for organizations and individuals, suggesting steps like establishing clear data governance policies, providing regular staff training on cybersecurity, promoting multi-factor authentication and encryption, and ensuring open lines for reporting potential threats. Embedding these practices into the fabric of an organization creates a stronger, more resilient system against cyber threats.

At the heart of preventing privacy breaches is the preservation of our fundamental right to privacy. In a time where our digital footprints are everywhere, protecting personal information is vital. It demands a joint effort from everyone—individuals, businesses, and governments—to advocate for digital privacy and strive for a safe, trustworthy online world. Ignoring this responsibility doesn't just hurt individuals; it shakes the very foundations of trust in society and the principles of democracy.

Chapter 5

Resistance Against Authoritarian Control

The spread of authoritarianism worldwide is more than a threat to personal freedoms and civil rights; it's an assault on democracy itself. This encroachment typically doesn't storm in with dramatic upheavals but creeps in slowly, undermining democratic institutions and values bit by bit, all under the pretext of ensuring stability or safeguarding national security. It thrives on dividing the people, making us fight amongst ourselves, playing on economic fears, and leveraging a diminishing trust in public dialogue, which paves the way for power to become more centralized.

What makes this situation even more challenging is the difficulty in spotting and standing up against these gradual shifts. Societies face the tough task of not only recognizing the early, often subtle signs of authoritarian tendencies but also crafting effective means to counter them. The lack of clear, momentous events signaling a move towards authoritarian governance means that any resistance must be thoughtful, forward-thinking, and grounded in both historical insight and an understanding of the present-day context. The rise of digital technologies adds another layer of complexity.

While these tools can aid in organizing and activism, they simultaneously provide authoritarian governments sophisticated methods to monitor, censor, and skew information.

The power of unity in the face of authoritarian challenges can be nothing short of inspirational. This was evident during the Civil Rights Movement in the United States, where individuals from varied walks of life united under a common goal to abolish racial segregation and discrimination. Their strategy was not just about bringing diverse groups together; it also involved engaging in strategic nonviolent actions that successfully disrupted the existing norms, forcing the nation to pay attention and address long-standing injustices.

Nonviolent resistance has left a strong mark in history because it has been proven to work well and is seen as morally better than violent methods. Mahatma Gandhi from India is a great example of this. He showed how following truth and peaceful protests helped India gain freedom from British control. His actions teach us that real power doesn't always mean being physically strong, but it lies in the determination of people who strive for fairness and peace.

Mahatma Gandhi's role in India's fight for freedom showed how nonviolent civil disobedience was a powerful tool. He led movements, protests, and boycotts without resorting to violence, showing the British that India was united in its desire for independence. Gandhi's teachings emphasized the importance of truth, justice, and peaceful resistance as key principles to achieving their goals.

The strength of nonviolent actions lies in the courage and conviction of the people who participate in them. Peaceful protests, civil disobedience, and acts of resistance can create powerful movements that bring about change without causing harm. Gandhi's message resonates through time, showing that by staying true to their beliefs and avoiding violence, individuals and communities can overcome oppression and achieve their objectives peacefully.

The Arab Spring offered another potent illustration of how solidarity and collective determination can challenge oppressive regimes. The Arab Spring began with ordinary people in Tunisia and Egypt standing up against corruption and limitations on their freedoms. From these humble beginnings, the movement grew, spreading to other countries in the region. Citizens, hungry for change, came together to demand a better future for themselves and future generations.

The path to revolution was not easy. Those part of the Arab Spring movements faced significant obstacles, including violence and resistance from the established authorities. Despite these challenges, the collective determination of the people remained strong, propelling them forward in their quest for a more just society.

Against all odds, the unified actions of the citizens participating in the Arab Spring movements yielded remarkable results. They succeeded in overthrowing leaders who had held power for years through oppressive means. The persistence and resilience of the protestors demonstrated the power of solidarity in effecting significant change.

The events of the Arab Spring underline the transformative potential of unified protests and collective action. By banding together and voicing their grievances as one, individuals were able to shake the foundations of entrenched regimes. The reverberations of their united efforts were felt far and wide, sparking hope for a more democratic and inclusive future in the region.

Studying past resistance movements can help us fight against authoritarianism today. People trying to make changes now face challenges in a complex world with sophisticated adversarial tactics. But, successful resistance still comes down to working together, using peaceful methods, and strategic collaboration. Learning from the past is very important, but it's also important to apply those lessons to today's world and technology. For example, digital platforms are great for organizing and advocating, but they also bring risks like surveillance and misleading information. To handle these challenges, we need careful planning and working together inclusively.

Studying past movements is important for today's activists. They need to talk openly and work together with different groups, use technology wisely, and build leaders who show honesty, humility, and a strong belief in democratic values. This kind of leadership builds trust and encourages people to keep taking part, even when difficult challenges arise.

The Pillars of Civil Society and Grassroots Organizations

At the heart of defending freedoms and pushing back against authoritarianism lie grassroots organizations and civil society. These groups are important because they give people a platform to support causes that fight for individual freedoms. By directly involving citizens, these movements help people feel empowered and actively participate in their communities. This is particularly important in places where authoritarian regimes aim to stifle opposition and restrict democratic engagement.

Grassroots movements play an essential role in keeping an eye on government actions, acting as guardians who hold authorities to account and shine a light on misuse of power. It's about making sure that the concerns of those who are often ignored are heard by those in charge, calling for transparency and justice. This role is especially vital where traditional media might be controlled or censored by government forces, leaving civil society as a key player in spreading information and rallying public opinion.

For both individuals and communities to stand strong against authoritarian overreach, getting involved and understanding civic responsibilities are key steps. Grassroots efforts lead the way in creating opportunities for learning about rights, governance, and participation in democracy. This kind of involvement cultivates a culture of active citizenship, providing people with the means to resist oppression and push for positive change. It further highlights how collective efforts can lead to significant shifts in society.

Additionally, emphasizing the inclusion of underrepresented voices and encouraging participatory decision-making are fundamental in strengthening defenses against authoritarianism. By bringing diverse perspectives into discussions on governance and policy, civil society guarantees broader representation and fortifies democratic principles. Making sure everyone, especially those who have been historically overlooked, gets to contribute to shaping their future, these organizations challenge authoritarian figures' attempts to monopolize power and mute dissent.

Civil society must stay up-to-date with the changing political landscape to make a difference. They need to understand how political shifts can affect their causes and adapt accordingly. It's important for grassroots activism and civil engagement to be aware of current political realities to make their efforts more effective.

Establishing strong connections between various civil society actors is imperative. By building networks, these groups can support each other, share valuable resources, and exchange ideas and strategies. This collaboration can lead to more impactful advocacy and activism initiatives.

Civil society actors should not work in isolation. By sharing resources such as funding, tools, and knowledge, they can enhance the impact of their work. Furthermore, exchanging strategies and insights can help organizations learn from each other's successes and failures, leading to more efficient and effective activism.

Strategic litigation plays a significant role in upholding human rights and democracy. By strategically using legal avenues to challenge unjust laws and actions, civil society can protect the rights of individuals and push back against oppressive measures. Drawing on both local and international legal standards can provide a solid foundation for these legal challenges. It is essential for civil society to stand against laws and actions that infringe upon human rights and democratic principles. By actively opposing such legislation through strategic litigation and advocacy efforts, these groups can uphold the values of justice, equality, and freedom. This proactive approach is essential in maintaining a just and democratic society.

Civil society actors should be well-versed in both domestic and international legal standards. By understanding and leveraging these legal frameworks, organizations can effectively challenge rights violations and undemocratic practices. This knowledge equips them to navigate legal processes and advocate for justice on various fronts.

These approaches underline the complex, rich tapestry of resistance against autocratic control. According to the International Center for Not-for-Profit Law (ICNL) in their overview of civil society's revival in authoritarian contexts (Odora, 2008), navigating the path toward democracy and safeguarding civil liberties is challenging. However, the perseverance and creativity shown by civil society groups worldwide provide hope and guidance for those dedicated to upholding democratic values and human rights.

Global Solidarity: A Networked Response to Authoritarianism

The role of international partnerships and support networks in protecting democracy cannot be underestimated. At the core of this strategy is the belief that there is strength in unity, especially when dealing with challenges that threaten democratic principles and human rights worldwide.

It's impressive how global community groups can help local resistance movements. These groups allow for sharing strategies, tools, and knowledge to make local movements known on a global scale. They play an important role in drawing worldwide attention to human rights violations that might otherwise be overlooked. By spotlighting these issues, global groups can pressure oppressive governments from the outside, providing support that is harder for these regimes to stop compared to internal opposition.

Moreover, international alliances play an important role in protecting activists confronting oppression in authoritarian states. These alliances, comprising various countries and international organizations, offer assistance such as asylum, legal support, and financial aid to activists who are targeted by their governments. This highlights the interconnected nature of democracy movements, demonstrating how the pursuit of freedom in one nation can impact the global fight for democracy.

At the foundation of cross-border partnerships are shared commitments to freedom and democracy. These common values lay the groundwork for diverse groups and nations to come together in their fight against authoritarian rule. When countries and organizations committed to democratic ideals join forces, they emphasize that democracy represents a fairer and more humane way forward for all. This united stance conveys a strong message against authoritarian practices and governance, underlining their misalignment with the worldwide aspiration for dignity, freedom, and human rights.

Forming coalitions and partnerships across national boundaries is vital for maintaining a united front to defend democracy. Activists, state representatives, and NGOs coming together can be a powerful force in safeguarding human rights and democratic principles. By combining their strengths and resources, these groups can effectively combat the rising influence of authoritarian regimes.

When activists, state representatives, and NGOs join forces, they create a network that protects human rights globally. This coalition can work towards ensuring that basic human rights are respected and upheld in all regions. By sharing information, strategies, and resources, they build a stronger defense mechanism against any threats to democracy.

The collaborative efforts of these groups enable a more robust response to the challenges posed by authoritarianism. By sharing intelligence and best practices, they can develop effective strategies to resist the spread of autocratic rule. Through this collective approach, they can confront authoritarian regimes and uphold democratic standards with greater efficacy.

Coalitions and partnerships allow for the exchange of ideas, strategies, and resources among diverse organizations. Activists, state representatives, and NGOs can benefit from shared knowledge and expertise, leading to more informed decision-making and coordinated action. This exchange of information enhances the collective capacity to address threats to democracy on a global scale.

The pooling of resources and influence through coalitions and partnerships strengthens the overall defense mechanism against threats to democracy. By leveraging their combined strengths, these entities can mount coordinated responses to challenges to democratic values. This collaborative approach increases their impact and resilience in the face of authoritarian pressures.

A unified front against threats to democracy is essential in today's interconnected world. Coalitions and partnerships play a pivotal role in bringing together diverse stakeholders under a common agenda. By fostering collaboration and mutual support, these alliances build a cohesive defense network that can effectively address emerging threats to democratic principles.

Through their collective efforts, these coalitions and partnerships work towards preserving democratic standards and upholding human rights globally. By advocating for democratic values and defending fundamental rights, they contribute to a more secure and democratic future for all. This commitment to unity and solidarity is essential in safeguarding the principles of democracy in a rapidly changing world.

The formation of coalitions and partnerships across borders is instrumental in protecting democracy and human rights. By uniting in a concerted effort, activists, state representatives, and NGOs can enhance their collective impact and resilience in the face of authoritarian challenges. Through cooperation, information sharing, and joint action, these entities can uphold democratic standards and counter threats to democracy effectively.

The world faces a growing challenge with the spread of authoritarianism on a global scale. Collaborative efforts and support from various nations are essential in addressing this concerning trend. Organizations such as Freedom House have extensively documented the rise of attacks on liberal democracy worldwide. This underscores the critical importance of democratic nations joining forces to push back against the creeping influence of authoritarian systems. The emergence of international alliances and networks of solidarity provides a beacon of hope, showcasing that by upholding shared values and working together, it is feasible to resist authoritarian incursions and champion democracy and human rights on a global scale.

Civic Engagement: The Foundation of Democratic Resilience

Democracy thrives not just on our right to cast a vote but on our active involvement in shaping society. This becomes especially pertinent as we face the growing influence of authoritarianism, which gradually infiltrates areas once illuminated by democratic values. Involvement in democratic practices, like voting and advocating for causes, is more than meeting a civic obligation. It's about reinforcing our liberties against the looming threat of tyranny.

Authoritarianism poses a threat that cannot be dealt with alone. Together, as a community, we can create strong defenses against misinformation and propaganda. By coming together, we can counter the tactics used by authoritarian governments, which rely on causing division among the people and spreading lies. Community events that promote open dialogue among different groups are crucial in this fight. When people from various backgrounds engage in discussions, they bring unique perspectives that challenge the falsehoods pushed by authoritarian regimes.

Imagine a neighborhood organizing a town hall meeting where residents, regardless of their backgrounds, gather to discuss current events and share their thoughts. Through these conversations, people learn from each other's experiences and beliefs, fostering unity and understanding. This unity becomes a shield against the divisive strategies of authoritarian leaders.

Another essential aspect of combating authoritarianism is enhancing media literacy and fact-checking skills. By improving our ability to discern reliable sources from false information, we empower ourselves and others to counteract deceptive narratives. Authenticating the information we consume allows us to uncover and challenge the misleading content perpetuated by authoritarian regimes. For instance, communities can organize workshops on media literacy, teaching participants how to evaluate sources, verify information, and distinguish between fact and fiction. By equipping individuals with these skills, we create a knowledgeable and vigilant society that can actively combat the spread of propaganda.

The strength of the collective effort lies in the diversity of perspectives it encompasses. When individuals unite to challenge authoritarian narratives, their varied viewpoints converge to form a formidable front against falsehoods. Embracing diversity within these efforts amplifies the impact of the resistance, demonstrating that a multitude of voices together can drown out the single narrative propagated by authoritarian regimes.

By ensuring that all voices are heard and respected, we cultivate an inclusive environment that celebrates differences while striving towards a common goal. Each perspective contributes a unique piece to the puzzle of resistance, enriching the movement with a tapestry of ideas and experiences.

Through community mobilization, media literacy enhancement, and the celebration of diverse viewpoints, we build a robust defense against authoritarian tactics. By fostering unity and understanding, equipping ourselves with critical skills, and embracing the strength of diversity, we create a powerful force capable of challenging and ultimately dismantling the deceptive narratives of authoritarianism.

Grassroots movements are a testament to the strength of democratic engagement and the quest for justice. They show us that impactful change often begins with small, local initiatives. These measures invigorate both individuals and communities, transforming them from passive observers into passionate champions of democracy.

At the heart of defending democratic norms is the promotion of a culture rich in civic responsibility and participation. To foster such an environment, we must implement civic education initiatives that highlight the significance of democratic values and the individual's role in preserving these ideals, and push for policies that make voting and public involvement more accessible, guaranteeing everyone's voice can be heard.

By cultivating a society that prioritizes active engagement, we fortify our defenses against efforts to weaken our freedoms, thereby securing democracy's future. The repercussions of these discussions stretch wide, touching not only those actively fighting for freedom and those shaping policy but also everyday people witnessing their freedoms being chipped away. More broadly, when democratic standards and ideals start to weaken, it poses a real risk to worldwide peace, stability, and the progress of humanity.

Chapter 6

The Nexus Between Governments and Big Tech Corporations

In today's world, the bond between tech companies and government policies plays a crucial role in shaping public opinion and how information flows. As we increasingly rely on digital platforms, their influence goes beyond just sharing data to become a key part of how society is run. This complex interaction brings up important issues such as the potential for companies to have too much influence over regulations, conflicts of interest, and how transparent these relationships are. Often, the balance between government rules and tech giants sways in ways that may not prioritize the public's needs, calling for a detailed examination of how these forces shape both our online and offline worlds.

The focus here is on how the power of corporations can sway laws and affect the creation of policies, impacting democracy itself. Instances where legislation seems to favor large technology companies raise concerns about whether the well-being of the public is being considered. The worry is that those responsible for regulating the digital space could be influenced by the very entities they're supposed to regulate. These situations make it challenging to address important issues like privacy, the spread of false information, and unfair market practices. The lines between those setting the rules and those following them become blurred, highlighting the urgent need to look closely at how tech behemoths can influence government actions for their benefit.

The relationship between governments and technology companies can be seen as a delicate dance, where both parties attempt to take the lead without fully considering whom they're performing for. At times, this interaction leans too much in favor of corporations due to regulatory capture—a situation that needs careful examination. Essentially, this term describes how tech giants can use their influence to sway policy decisions in their direction, often leaving the public interest sidelined.

Regulatory capture happens when the agencies meant to oversee certain industries end up being influenced by those very sectors. This creates a scenario akin to letting the fox guard the henhouse, where legislation tends to benefit large tech firms over the needs of the general populace. This issue is not just speculative; David Dayen (2023) pointed out that lobbyists from major tech industries have successfully changed how trade negotiations view technology platforms and their policies, indicating a shift towards policies that prioritize industry benefits over public welfare.

As we explore the consequences of conflicting interests in technology management, it becomes evident that the lines between regulators and the regulated are becoming increasingly blurred. This lack of distinction impacts transparency and accountability, making it challenging to comprehend technology's societal effects and address critical issues like data privacy and monopolistic practices.

To mitigate big tech's disproportionate influence on governmental decisions, it's vital to establish stronger regulatory measures. Steps toward fairer outcomes include setting up independent oversight bodies resistant to corporate lobbying, implementing clear conflict-of-interest guidelines for individuals transitioning between the tech sector and government roles, and conducting regular policy audits to ensure they serve the public interest. Moreover, involving the public and non-profit organizations in policy discussions can help balance out industry perspectives.

Recognizing instances of regulatory capture in the tech industry requires constant vigilance and a dedication to openness. For those invested in protecting our digital environment, here are some actions to consider: increasing awareness about how regulatory capture works and its effects, supporting reform initiatives in tech governance, insisting on accountability from tech firms and regulatory bodies alike, and promoting investigative work that examines the ties between tech magnates and government entities.

Encouraging a culture of scrutiny and high standards in policy formulation can help reduce the dangers linked to regulatory capture and interest conflicts. An informed and active community serves as an effective check against the undermining of democratic principles by corporate powers. In managing the intricate dynamics between technology and government, it's crucial to remember what's at risk—the essence of our digital existence. Allowing policy to be dictated by a select few risks stifling innovation, compromising privacy, and widening the digital divide.

The path we're on is changeable. Through advocacy for transparent, responsible, and participatory policy-making, technology can become a force for empowerment and advancement rather than a means for narrow profit-making. The hurdles are substantial, yet they can be overcome with determination and collective action.

Corporate Censorship and Public Discourse

Exploring the tricky relationship between how companies control online content and its effect on what we talk about, it's key to first look at why businesses might decide to limit access to certain information. The main issue lies in finding a middle ground between making the internet a safe place and allowing people to freely express their thoughts. Businesses are motivated by various factors, such as following the law or maintaining a good image, which puts them in a tough spot. They have to figure out how to filter content to shield users from what they deem as 'harmful material' without stepping on individuals' rights too much. This balancing act raises questions about how these choices influence the variety of opinions and information we see online.

Turning our attention to how controlling content affects things, we notice that its impact goes way beyond just getting rid of dangerous material. The very act of filtering information can change how ideas and information circulate, possibly limiting the range of voices we hear. Such a system could unintentionally push aside lesser-heard voices or unpopular opinions. It highlights a complex issue in managing digital spaces that calls for clear and fair rules in handling online content.

Social Media companies like Facebook, Twitter, Reddit, and YouTube have been increasingly censoring opposing views in recent years. Among these, YouTube has gained notoriety for its strict censorship practices. Users and content creators who express opinions contrary to the platform's beliefs are promptly censored. An example of this censorship occurred during the COVID-19 pandemic. Individuals who merely suggested the virus may have originated from the Wuhan Institute of Virology in China faced immediate consequences. Their videos were demonetized or deleted, comments were censored, and some users even had their accounts suspended. These actions were taken despite the fact that the lab leak hypothesis is now widely acknowledged by experts globally.

The impact of censorship on social media platforms can be significant. Content creators and users who provide valuable perspectives or critical thinking may be discouraged from sharing their views due to fear of censorship. When platforms suppress differing viewpoints, they limit the diversity of ideas and opinions that users are exposed to. This can create echo chambers where only one narrative is permitted, stifling meaningful discourse and intellectual growth.

Maintaining open dialogue and allowing for a variety of perspectives is very important for a healthy online community. When individuals are free to express their ideas, engage in respectful debates, and challenge existing beliefs, it fosters a culture of intellectual curiosity and growth. Platforms that prioritize open dialogue empower users to think critically, form informed opinions, and contribute to a more vibrant and inclusive digital space.

Protecting freedom of expression is essential in upholding democracy and individual liberties. Censorship by tech companies raises concerns about the suppression of free speech and the silencing of dissenting voices. Users should have the right to express their opinions, share information responsibly, and engage in constructive conversations without the fear of censorship or reprisal. Upholding freedom of expression fosters a culture of transparency, accountability, and mutual respect within online communities.

While moderation is necessary to maintain a safe and respectful online environment, it is essential for tech companies to strike a balance between moderation and freedom of expression. Implementing transparent moderation policies, providing clear guidelines for acceptable content, and fostering open communication between users and platforms can help mitigate censorship concerns. By prioritizing fairness, inclusivity, and accountability, tech companies can cultivate an online ecosystem that values diverse perspectives and promotes constructive dialogue.

As online platforms continue to evolve, the debate surrounding censorship, freedom of expression, and content moderation is likely to intensify. Finding common ground that respects individual rights while addressing concerns related to harmful content and misinformation will be vital for shaping the future of online discourse. Collaborative efforts between tech companies, policymakers, users, and advocacy groups can pave the way for a more equitable and inclusive digital landscape where freedom of expression is upheld, diverse voices are welcomed, and meaningful conversations thrive.

Finding a good balance involves talking openly while dealing with the risks of online content. It's a difficult challenge because of the ever-changing nature of the web. The main issue is figuring out how to support free speech while also handling problems like false information, hate speech, and other harmful content. To do this, we need to watch carefully and make sure that the online space is good for having meaningful conversations.

Looking at solutions, platforms can take concrete actions to ensure their policies on content align better with democratic ideals. Steps include setting up strong systems for users to appeal decisions, being transparent about why some content is removed, and working closely with various groups to shape policies. Moreover, it's vital for platforms to clearly explain their guidelines and decision-making to users. Doing so helps improve public discussion, bridging the gap in understanding and expectations between users and the platform.

Regulatory rules are important for guiding content management. A big challenge is making laws that handle harmful content without limiting free speech. Following the guidelines from the Office of the High Commissioner for Human Rights (OHCHR) seems like a good idea. This way focuses on making sure actions are legal, necessary, and fair when controlling online content. This encourages both countries and corporations to improve moderation methods instead of putting restrictions on specific content.

For a more balanced approach, steps can be taken to ensure that any restrictions on online content are legally justified, necessary to safeguard interests like public health or safety, and does not interfere with free expression. Advocating for increased transparency from platforms regarding their content management policies assists users in understanding the reasoning behind decisions. Backing the establishment and utilization of channels for users to contest content rulings guarantees accessibility, fairness, and efficiency in these processes. Promoting collaboration among governments, civil organizations, tech firms, and other stakeholders to establish standards and best practices for responsible content management that upholds human rights and cultivates lively public discussions.

Surveillance, Privacy, and Control

The point where government oversight meets private data gathering forms a complicated area that often sees our privacy rights getting overshadowed. Both government bodies and private corporations are collecting heaps of information, making it hard to distinguish between actions taken for national security and those that cross into invading our personal space. It's important to examine the overlap of these activities and their impact on our privacy.

There is a complex bond between governments and big tech companies, with data acting as the currency of exchange. This relationship has led to an unparalleled level of information gathering, sparking major privacy concerns. Many people feel uneasy about the way our data is scooped up and used by both state entities and businesses. This discomfort comes from knowing that every click and online movement might be watched, dissected, and possibly exploited without our consent.

At the core of this issue lies the merging of government surveillance with private sector data mining efforts, presenting a sophisticated challenge to our privacy rights. Governments claim they need data access for things like fighting terrorism and stopping crime, while tech firms gather personal details promising better services and tailored ads. Although their reasons differ greatly, the outcome is a deep invasion of personal privacy.

This invasion becomes even more tangled due to ethical questions tied to the partnership between governments and tech companies for data collection. Such cooperation affects how people view these institutions and can lead to distrust and a feeling of disappointment. Knowing that one's data might be used for more than originally thought, such as targeted ads or, more worryingly, measures for social manipulation, highlights the need for a closer look at this alliance.

Data sharing has become a significant issue in discussions about social control. The act of sharing data is not just about passing information between individuals or entities; it is also about the power dynamics at play. When data is shared, it can be used to shape narratives, influence behavior, and monitor opposition. This ability to analyze data gives both governments and large companies immense control over individuals and populations. For instance, if a government collects data on its citizens' browsing habits, it can potentially manipulate the information to control how people perceive certain events or ideas.

Recent studies, such as those conducted by the Pew Research Center, have shown that many Americans are wary of data gathering practices by governmental agencies and corporations. The general sentiment is that the risks associated with data sharing outweigh any potential benefits. This concern is rooted in the fear that personal information could be misused to manipulate individuals. Whether through targeted advertising strategies or more direct forms of social influence, the idea of data being weaponized against people is a pervasive worry.

The notion that data sharing can lead to social control is not unfounded. In today's digital age, information is power. By collecting and analyzing vast amounts of data, organizations can craft tailored messages that sway public opinion. For example, social media platforms utilize user data to display specific content, influencing users' beliefs and behaviors. This practice blurs the line between informed choices and manipulative tactics, raising questions about the ethical implications of data-driven control mechanisms.

Privacy concerns are at the forefront of discussions on data sharing and social control. Individuals are increasingly aware of the risks posed by sharing personal information online. The fear of data misuse has led to calls for more stringent privacy regulations and oversight. Without proper safeguards in place, the potential for data to be exploited for nefarious purposes remains a pressing issue. Protecting privacy rights becomes essential in the face of growing data collection practices that have the capacity to infringe on personal freedoms.

Addressing the complexities of data sharing requires a reevaluation of consent and transparency standards. Users must be fully informed about how their data is collected, stored, and utilized. Transparent data practices empower individuals to make informed decisions about sharing their information. Moreover, obtaining explicit consent for data processing activities is essential in upholding ethical standards. By enhancing transparency and consent frameworks, organizations can mitigate concerns around social control and data manipulation.

One way to address fears surrounding data sharing and social control is to enhance data security measures. Implementing robust cybersecurity protocols can safeguard against unauthorized access and data breaches. Organizations must prioritize data protection to prevent sensitive information from falling into the wrong hands. By investing in secure encryption methods and regularly updating security protocols, the risks associated with data sharing can be minimized, fostering trust among users and mitigating concerns over social control.

Promoting data literacy and awareness is key to navigating the complexities of data sharing in the context of social control. Individuals need to understand the implications of sharing their personal data online and the potential consequences of data misuse. Education initiatives aimed at improving data literacy can empower individuals to protect their privacy rights and make informed choices about data sharing practices. By fostering a culture of data awareness, society can better navigate the evolving landscape of data-driven control mechanisms.

Recognizing these anxieties, it's critical to think about ways to shield personal data from unsanctioned access. Keeping personal details safe in today's digital world involves a blend of clever technology use and legal changes. People can protect themselves by encrypting data, being cautious about what they share online, and carefully choosing what data they allow apps to access. Yet, it's clear that individual efforts alone aren't enough.

Addressing the challenges posed by data sharing and social control requires collaborative efforts from various stakeholders. Advocacy groups, policymakers, and industry leaders play an important role in shaping data governance policies that prioritize user privacy and security. By advocating for transparent data practices and supporting stronger data protection laws, stakeholders can work together to create a more ethical and accountable data sharing environment. Collaboration is essential in fostering a collective commitment to upholding individuals' rights in the face of expanding data control mechanisms.

Updating laws to match digital advancements is paramount to build strong data protection structures. We need clear regulations that make governments and companies transparent and accountable for how they handle data. It's also vital to have strict rules around consent, giving people back control over their personal information. Educating everyone on digital know-how will equip them to make smarter choices about their online presence and understand the risks involved.

These steps are essential in lessening the dangers brought by the mix of state surveillance and private data collection. With such actions, we aim for a future where technological progress doesn't sacrifice our fundamental right to privacy.

Monopolistic Power and Its Democratic Impact

The swift ascent of big tech companies has dramatically changed our digital world, highlighting critical issues about their effect on democracy. The core problem is the immense control these firms have over information and ideas, which can limit competition and creativity, threatening democracy's very foundation.

The power a few corporations hold to dictate the news and information accessible to billions of people raises significant concerns for democratic dialogue. By manipulating what appears in news feeds, promoting certain perspectives over others, and silencing opposing voices through their policies, these companies not only restrict consumer choices but also subtly influence public opinion and political outcomes.

Moreover, the concentration of technological power influences societal trends, affecting everything from what we buy to how we vote. Social media platforms, in particular, create environments where opposing views can be overshadowed by the most popular or loudest opinions, hindering constructive, democratic conversations.

Tackling these intricate challenges requires meticulous consideration. Regulators and policymakers must strike a delicate balance between promoting fair competition and innovation while safeguarding democratic principles. A fundamental approach may involve modernizing antitrust statutes to tackle the specific hurdles of the digital economy, such as data management and dominance within platforms, to ensure equitable opportunities for smaller tech companies.

It's also vital to boost civic participation to overcome these hurdles. People should be equipped with the skills to critically assess information, understand how digital platforms work, and hold both governments and companies accountable. Enhancing digital literacy is very important here, preparing citizens to effectively engage with the digital world.

To address the problem of big tech companies controlling too much and protect democracy, we should encourage standards that are open to everyone and systems that work well together. Backing independent media and journalism can help balance out the power of tech giants over what information we get. It's important to use technology in a responsible way and make sure it's developed with ethics and how it will affect society in mind for the long term. It's important to join conversations and work with others around the world to deal with how much power digital platforms have and come up with unified plans.

Throughout our exploration of these important matters at the intersection of technology and governance, it's evident that the balance of power is fluid and can be reshaped. The journey toward reform and positive change begins with a deep understanding and proactive approach to these issues. It serves as a call to action for government officials, policymakers, activists, scholars, and concerned individuals to collaborate towards establishing a digital environment marked by transparency, accountability, and inclusivity.

Thinking about what's at stake, it becomes obvious that failing to act—or acting carelessly—has repercussions that ripple through society, affecting us all. We stand before an uncertain future, akin to a blank canvas. It's up to us, through collective effort, creativity, and ethical leadership, to paint a picture where technology serves as a force for empowerment rather than a tool for tyranny.

Chapter 7

Citizen Empowerment in the Face of Tyranny

In today's world, where we spend much of our time online, it's harder than ever to tell what's true and what's not. This murky situation is perfect for authoritarian governments who use confusion to their advantage. They spread false stories and use the internet for spying, all of which threatens our freedom and democracy.

The issue goes deeper than just knowing how to spot a fake news story. It's about understanding why people might share these stories in the first place, even when they have facts that say otherwise. People often prefer information that fits what they already believe, a tendency known as confirmation bias. When authoritarian groups manipulate information, this problem gets even trickier. It shows us just how complicated the battle against misinformation is, highlighting the need for a well-rounded plan that not only sharpens our critical thinking but also shapes our moral values online.

Digital literacy and the ability to think critically aren't just trendy terms in education; they're vital for helping us sift through the vast amount of information we come across online every day. In a world where it's getting harder to tell real news from fake, these skills are more important than ever. They help us evaluate the reliability of different sources and decide what to believe. But it's more than that — these skills encourage us to question and analyze information instead of just taking it at face value. This critical approach is key in fighting misinformation and propaganda, which are often used by authoritarian regimes to shape public opinion.

Being savvy about the digital world helps us protect our online privacy and security, but there's more to it. Real digital literacy means understanding how digital platforms operate and the impact they can have on us. It plays an important role in defending against surveillance and censorship, tactics used by those who want to limit freedom and control the flow of information. To boost your digital literacy, try adopting safe communication methods, using encryption for sensitive information, and staying up to date with privacy settings on social media. Taking these steps helps you maintain your right to privacy in a world that's constantly connected.

Promoting digital literacy broadly helps create a society of informed and active citizens. It encourages folks to not just passively absorb content but to actively engage with it, asking where it came from and understanding its context. This kind of environment supports democratic participation and stands as a defense against authoritarian narratives built on misinformation and unchallenged claims. When people can critically assess information, they're in a better position to make smart choices, partake in meaningful conversations, and hold leaders accountable.

But in today's digital age, critical thinking goes beyond spotting reliable information. An essential part of protecting ourselves from false information is verifying facts before sharing them online. Sharing incorrect stories can lead to confusion or even serious issues affecting public health and safety. Developing a habit of checking facts with numerous trusted sources or fact-checking sites is not just about avoiding personal missteps; it's about responsibly contributing to the online community and not spreading questionable statements. "This practice is not only about reducing personal susceptibility to misinformation but also about contributing responsibly to the digital ecosystem by not amplifying dubious claims" (MIT Sloan, n.d.).

However, simply spreading digital literacy won't solve the problem of misinformation altogether. Research shows that even those well-versed in digital tools can end up sharing false information. This reveals the complicated nature of human psychology and the strong pull of confirmation bias—our tendency to embrace information that supports what we already believe. While digital literacy can improve our ability to distinguish between truth and lies, ultimately, whether we share information might depend more on deep-seated cognitive biases. That's why it's important to work on shifting our mindset towards valuing accuracy over personal beliefs when deciding what to share online.

Encouraging digital literacy and critical thinking doesn't just protect us against propaganda. It builds a society resilient enough to resist efforts by authoritarian forces to erode democratic principles and human rights. By continually educating ourselves and engaging in promoting these skills, we're not just navigating the digital world more effectively; we're also asserting our dedication to preserving the truthfulness of our shared information space.

Legal Frameworks and Human Rights

In our goal to protect democratic ideals from the threat of authoritarian rule, it's important to understand and put to use legal structures along with human rights tools. These resources provide individuals with the knowledge needed to identify when their freedoms are at risk and offer ways to challenge and rectify such violations.

A key first step is to demystify the intricate realm of human rights instruments. These agreements represent a global understanding on norms safeguarding personal freedom and dignity. For effective use of these tools, one must familiarize themselves with various treaties, declarations, and conventions, such as the Universal Declaration of Human Rights and the International Covenant on Civil and Political Rights.

To improve understanding, one might choose to explore materials from reputable human rights organizations and participate in workshops or online courses focused on human rights law. Observing how cases are presented before international human rights bodies can provide insights into the structure of legal arguments and the assertion of rights. This dedication to learning enriches awareness of universal rights and equips individuals to confidently address violations.

Navigating the legal system becomes easier when you grow your legal knowledge, whether it's within your country or on a global scale. It's imperative to know what your rights are under your country's constitution and how international human rights standards are relevant in local contexts. One way to simplify this process is by studying significant legal decisions in your area that pertain to human rights matters. Seek advice from experts in human rights to help you understand complex legal concepts better. Building relationships with advocacy organizations that provide legal education can greatly assist in safeguarding your civil liberties. By being familiar with legal precedents and knowing the available legal avenues, you can make more informed decisions when faced with illegal actions by authorities.

Consulting legal specialists in the field of human rights can provide valuable insights into the legal intricacies that affect you. These experts can explain legal doctrines and principles in a way that is easier to understand, giving you a better grasp of how the law applies to your situation. By seeking guidance from human rights specialists, individuals can gain confidence in their knowledge of legal rights and protections.

Getting involved with advocacy groups that focus on legal education is beneficial for staying informed about your rights. These organizations often offer workshops, seminars, and resources that can enhance your understanding of human rights laws. By joining such groups, you can connect with like-minded individuals who are passionate about protecting civil liberties. Attending events and discussions organized by these advocacy groups can provide practical insights on how to defend your rights effectively.

Studying landmark legal cases related to human rights issues can deepen your understanding of legal principles and their practical applications. By analyzing how courts have interpreted and enforced laws in the past, you can anticipate potential legal outcomes in similar situations. Understanding legal precedents equips you with the knowledge needed to respond strategically to unjust practices or governmental interventions. Knowing how previous cases have shaped legal interpretations empowers individuals to make well-informed decisions when advocating for their rights.

Armed with knowledge of legal precedents and resources provided by human rights organizations, individuals can develop proactive strategies to address legal challenges. By being aware of the options available through judicial systems and alternative dispute resolution mechanisms, you can prepare for potential legal disputes or infringements on your rights. Creating a proactive response plan based on legal insights and precedents can enhance your ability to defend your rights effectively.

Collaborating with legal experts, human rights advocates, and community organizations can amplify your impact when dealing with legal issues. By leveraging the expertise of professionals in the field and pooling resources with individuals with shared perspectives, you can strengthen your advocacy efforts. Seeking guidance from legal professionals and engaging with diverse stakeholders can lead to more comprehensive approaches to addressing legal challenges and promoting human rights protections. By actively participating in legal education initiatives and advocacy campaigns, individuals can contribute to broader efforts aimed at upholding civil liberties and promoting justice.

Though acquiring legal knowledge may seem overwhelming, it's important to recognize its vital role in empowerment. Knowledge indeed equals power—being informed about legal protections enhances our autonomy. It motivates active involvement in community matters, from casting votes to participating in protests, backed by the understanding that there are legal foundations supporting these activities. This not only aids the individual but also bolsters the collective determination to stand against power misuse.

Moreover, advocating for civil liberties through legal avenues is essential in preserving democracy's defenses. It goes beyond retaliating against overreaches; it includes proactive initiatives to broaden and reinforce everyone's guaranteed protections. Efforts like grassroots movements, public campaigns, and lobbying are critical. They spotlight deficiencies in legal rights protection and advocate for adjustments ensuring domestic laws comply with international human rights norms. Collective efforts can counter authoritarian tendencies, keeping democratic values strong and secure.

The analysis by Freedom House brings attention to the current critical moment concerning internet freedom—a field increasingly under human rights scrutiny. Their suggestions underline the need to guard privacy, ensure safety, and uphold free speech online. These recommendations reflect a larger call for attentiveness and proactive engagement in protecting freedoms in our digital era. As global internet liberty wanes, putting these advisories into practice becomes even more relevant. It emphasizes the requirement for cooperation among individuals, policy makers, and tech firms to keep the digital realm a place where democracy and human rights can thrive.

Promoting Democratic Values

Education is a cornerstone for nurturing a strong democracy. Through teaching young minds about the importance of civic duty and democratic values, we instill in them a deep-rooted commitment to freedom, equality, and collective responsibility. This early education on democratic ethos prepares individuals to effectively defend their rights against authoritarianism.

Central to transforming education to support democracy is civic education. These programs go beyond just knowing how the government works or memorizing parts of the constitution. They aim to instill a deep respect for human rights, inspire active participation in democracy, and highlight the critical role of tolerance and diversity in a thriving society. Education reforms that include discussions on current events, promote critical thinking, and encourage student-led community projects significantly enhance students' appreciation and understanding of democratic values.

For these educational reforms to take root, certain strategies must be implemented. Civic education should encompass a wide range of topics such as the significance of voting, understanding the checks and balances system to prevent tyranny, and appreciating the value of civil liberties. Schools need to offer students practical experiences in democracy, like involvement in school governance or community service, to solve real-world issues. Teachers should be trained to facilitate open discussions, embrace diverse opinions, and cultivate an environment where debate and questioning are integral to learning.

Spreading awareness about democratic values and encouraging citizen participation isn't confined to the classroom. It extends to community activities where people can gather to address local issues. Through public forums, town hall meetings, and social media campaigns, communities can forge a shared dedication to democratic principles. Such participatory actions help citizens gain a deeper understanding of democracy and its challenges, strengthening our democratic fabric by affirming the significance of every voice and vote.

Empowering individuals with education is vital in defending democracy. An educated populous acts as the foundation on which a strong society is built. Education that sharpens critical thinking, fosters empathy, and broadens understanding of global challenges equips people to reject authoritarian ideologies. It develops thoughtful individuals who can discern misinformation and oppose unfair practices. Furthermore, by valuing pluralism and diversity, education stands as a bulwark against divisiveness. Higher education institutions play a vital role here; as centers for innovation and inquiry, they're perfectly placed to champion democratic ideals and drive social change.

By weaving democratic values into our education system, we foster a culture of respect and tolerance from a young age. Initiating this socialization process early sets the stage for a society that upholds human rights and equality. This method not only challenges authoritarian narratives but also celebrates the power of diversity and inclusive conversation. In short, an education geared towards democracy equips future leaders with the ethical guidance needed to tackle today's societal challenges while remaining steadfast in their democratic convictions.

The impact of integrating democratic values into education and promoting active citizenship is profound. It lays down the groundwork for a populace that is engaged, informed, and resilient. These measures ensure that democracy remains dynamic and strong, ready to face authoritarian threats. The takeaway is unmistakable: educational and awareness initiatives are vital in safeguarding democracy. They equip individuals with the essential knowledge, skills, and values for protecting their rights and actively participating in the democratic dialogue.

Grassroots Movements and Advocacy

Grassroots movements are the lifeblood of democracy, buzzing with the energy of citizens who band together to push their communities toward more control and fairness. This collective effort is incredibly powerful—ordinary people join forces, showing that they can take on authoritarian powers and push for changes that make society more democratic. The fact that these movements are not tied down by heavy layers of bureaucracy means they can quickly adapt to new challenges as they arise.

The importance of people getting involved in these movements cannot be overstressed. When individuals actively participate, they don't just raise their own voices; they help shape conversations that influence policies at all levels of government. It's a critical way to ensure leaders are held accountable, helping keep democracy and human rights secure.

To make grassroots campaigns even stronger, certain strategies are essential. One key tactic is making the most of social media platforms like Twitter and Facebook. These tools are great for organizing support and spreading the word, turning online spaces into hubs of civic activity.

Additionally, running an advocacy campaign takes careful planning. This involves setting clear goals that resonate with the community, bringing together a wide range of supporters for more impact, and sharing stories that personally connect with people and bring the cause to life.

Forming partnerships with organizations and individuals who share your vision can also fortify efforts against authoritarian challenges. Such alliances create a sturdy network that defends common principles, amplifying the message and ensuring a wider range of voices gets heard in pursuit of change.

At its core, grassroots activism is about giving people the power to believe they can make a difference. By tackling issues directly within their communities through local projects or discussions, individuals get a real taste of what activism feels like. This practical involvement reveals how major change often starts with small, community-based steps.

Through countless examples around the globe, the tremendous role of grassroots movements in driving social and political reform has been clearly demonstrated ("The Power of Grassroots Movements in Political Change | Good Party, n.d."). The lessons learned from historical successes serve as both motivation and a guide for today's activists, highlighting how united actions can challenge injustices and advocate for policies that reflect the community's desires over authoritarian dictates.

However, the path of grassroots movements is filled with hurdles such as keeping up the momentum and maneuvering through complex political terrains. But the achievements to date confirm that when people unite behind a common goal, armed with knowledge and tools, they have the potential to truly transform societies. These movements showcase democracy in action—not just in governmental halls but in the daily lives of those brave enough to envision a more open and just world.

Keeping the spirit of activism alive requires constant attention. The initial excitement can diminish in the face of obstacles or slow progress. To keep everyone engaged and motivated, it's important to communicate regularly, celebrate every win, no matter how small, and build a strong sense of belonging among members.

It can be difficult to find the right balance between local projects and bigger goals. Local efforts do really well in communities by using local connections to handle specific problems. But to make these actions have an impact on a national or global scale, it's important to team up with others strategically. These partnerships can connect local projects with larger objectives, making the whole movement much stronger.

Despite these challenges, grassroots movements remain a force for incredible change, impacting everything from environmental policies to equal rights. They've proven time and again their ability to shift public opinion, influence policy, and redefine what's possible.

The Power of Unity

When individuals unite, we harness the ability to shape the destinies of our communities. This power is not to be underestimated, as every voice added strengthens the collective impact. For instance, in a neighborhood plagued by safety concerns, the community can organize a neighborhood watch program where each person plays a vital role in ensuring the well-being of all residents. Through teamwork and collaboration, a sense of security can be established, making the community a safer place to live.

Furthermore, the unity of people extends far beyond the confines of immediate communities. At a global level, collective action can address pressing issues, such as climate change. By participating in initiatives like community clean-up events, individuals contribute to the greater environmental movement. Small acts, when combined, lead to significant changes, demonstrating how unity can drive impactful transformations on a larger scale.

The strength of unity lies in the numbers that stand together in solidarity. Consider a community coming together to support a local charity event. Each individual contribution, whether through volunteer work or donations, adds to the overall success of the initiative. This strength in numbers not only boosts the morale of participants but also amplifies the positive outcomes achieved through collaborative efforts.

Unity fosters the building of meaningful relationships among individuals within a community. Through shared experiences and common goals, bonds are formed that transcend individual differences. For example, a community garden project can bring together people from diverse backgrounds who share a passion for gardening. Working side by side, participants learn from one another, forging connections that enrich their lives beyond the project itself.

When people unite, their voices become louder and more impactful. This amplification is evident in advocacy campaigns aimed at addressing social injustices. By standing together and advocating for change, individuals can challenge systemic issues and bring about meaningful reforms. Each voice adds to the chorus of calls for justice, making it harder to ignore the collective demands of the community.

Unity celebrates the diversity within communities and recognizes the strength that comes from embracing differences. In multicultural neighborhoods, festivals that showcase various traditions and cuisines bring residents together in a spirit of unity. These celebrations serve to honor the unique contributions of each individual while fostering a sense of unity that transcends cultural divides.

In times of adversity, unity serves as a source of strength and resilience for communities facing challenges. When natural disasters strike, communities that come together to support one another demonstrate unwavering resilience. From organizing relief efforts to providing emotional support, unity enables communities to weather the storm and emerge stronger in the face of adversity.

Unity has the power to transform communities and societies by fostering collaboration, amplifying voices, and celebrating diversity. Through collective action, individuals can address pressing issues, build meaningful relationships, and overcome challenges with resilience. By recognizing the strength that comes from unity, we pave the way for a brighter, more inclusive future for all.

Chapter 8

The Psychological Impact of Authoritarianism

Living in a country ruled by an authoritarian government affects more than just its politics—it profoundly impacts how people feel on the inside. When facts are twisted and everyone is constantly watched, fear starts to feel normal. People become very cautious about what they say and do, always on the lookout for dangers that might not even be visible. This kind of atmosphere leads to distrust among community members, slowly deteriorating the connections that keep societies intact. As people's freedoms decrease, their ability to be themselves and make independent choices also diminishes.

The mental toll of living this way is significant and widespread. Being constantly enveloped in fear and control can severely damage mental health, causing more people to experience anxiety, depression, and a deep sense of hopelessness. When individuals have no control over their own thoughts and actions, it can lead to a profound feeling of being trapped. People are not only fighting against the limits placed on them from the outside but are also dealing with the struggle of losing their sense of self and personal beliefs. This doesn't just hurt individuals; it disrupts the unity and strength of entire communities under authoritarian control.

However, understanding how authoritarian governments use fear and suppression to control populations marks the first step towards reducing their damaging psychological effects. We must look into ways to build resilience and protect mental health in oppressive environments. Embracing critical thinking, establishing secure ways to communicate freely, and supporting each other within the community are key strategies in this fight. By enabling people to regain some control over their lives and thoughts, we lay the groundwork for resistance against authoritarian rule. Collective efforts and solidarity can help weaken the grip of fear, making room for a future where individuals can live with freedom and respect.

Transitioning from an awareness of the tactics used by oppressive regimes to actively counteracting their impact involves mobilizing around vital survival mechanisms. Secure communication platforms play an essential role in this process, allowing for the exchange of ideas and fostering a sense of community among those who are otherwise isolated by fear. Building networks that prioritize safety and confidentiality enables individuals to share experiences and strategies without the risk of reprisal. This collective wisdom becomes a powerful tool in combating the isolation and disempowerment that often accompany authoritarian governance.

Moreover, engaging in community support activities offers both practical and emotional benefits. Participating in organized groups helps to distribute the weight of oppression, making it more manageable for individuals. These groups can provide essential resources, ranging from psychological support to guidance on navigating the challenges posed by restrictive regimes. Furthermore, community initiatives can serve as a beacon of hope, reminding people that they are not alone in their struggles. The act of coming together in face of adversity reinforces social bonds and builds a collective resilience that can withstand the pressures of authoritarianism.

As we explore this issue further, the emphasis on empowering individuals and communities highlights the potential for change even under the most challenging circumstances. Fostering environments where free thought and expression are valued and protected is fundamental in mitigating the psychological strain imposed by authoritarianism. It also serves as a reminder that the human spirit is incredibly resilient. With the right tools and a shared commitment to liberty and dignity, overcoming the shadow of oppressive regimes is within reach.

Understanding Mechanisms of Fear and Control

In countries where authoritarian leaders hold power, these figures often use fear as a tool to keep everyone in line. They spread massive amounts of propaganda and watch people's every move. This approach deeply affects how people think and feel. Propaganda twists information to support a certain political goal, sometimes stretching the truth or making false claims. This flood of misleading information makes it hard for folks to tell what's real from what's not, creating a climate of fear over threats that may or may not exist.

Meanwhile, surveillance takes this fear to a whole new level, seeping into all aspects of life. Knowing that someone might always be watching or listening causes significant stress. This feeling of being watched all the time chips away at personal privacy and independence. People start to watch what they say and do – not just in public, but in private, too, and eventually, even their thoughts are influenced. This leads to an environment where free and open communication is replaced by silence, self-censorship, or simply repeating what authorities say.

The loss of freedom and autonomy has deep psychological effects. When people can't trust their own opinions, rely on their view of reality, or speak freely, they can feel powerless. This mistrust extends to institutions connected to the authoritarian regime, disrupting social harmony and the basic agreements that hold communities together. Furthermore, the constant stress can result in serious mental health problems, like depression, anxiety, and ongoing stress.

However, understanding how authoritarian leaders maintain control isn't just about recognizing the difficulties faced by those under such regimes; it opens doors for fighting back. Realizing the tactics of fear and control gives people the tools to regain control in oppressive settings. By examining these methods, individuals can come up with strategies that lessen the psychological burdens of living under authoritarian rule, building resilience and unity within affected groups.

A key strategy to counteract the mind games of authoritarian governments is to promote critical thinking towards media. Teaching folks to critically assess the information they come across, spotting bias and propaganda, can loosen the hold of fear-driven stories. Similarly, creating trusted networks for sharing information offers different perspectives that challenge the single narrative pushed by authoritarian figures.

Additionally, developing spaces, whether online or physical, where people can speak freely and share their stories acts as a defense against the loneliness and division intended through surveillance and censorship. Sharing experiences of oppression, utilizing platforms that take a strong stance against censorship, can turn feelings of isolation into a sense of solidarity, spurring group action or offering emotional support to each other.

Dealing with the mental impacts of living under authoritarian rule involves each person's determination and group effort. It means understanding and fighting against tactics of fear and control, while also supporting a culture that values freedom, critical thinking, and community help. By doing this, we can start to break free from the mental chains of authoritarianism and regain the freedoms that are vital for our dignity.

Surveillance, Repression, and Individual Autonomy

Living in a place ruled by an iron fist changes everything about everyday life. The endless monitoring and squashing of any dissent shrink the space for personal freedom, making it hard for people to freely express themselves. It's like being watched all the time, creating a climate where fear rules and people start to censor their own words. Imagine having to be careful with every word you say, knowing that even the slightest slip could get you in trouble. Under these conditions, trust becomes rare as doubt creeps into friendships and community connections, corrupting them from the inside.

Furthermore, the constant state of being watched does more than just break down trust; it builds walls of isolation around people. When there's always a chance someone might report something as simple as a complaint or an offhand comment, choosing silence becomes the safer path. This retreat can take a heavy toll on one's mental well-being, breeding paranoia and loneliness. Feeling like you're always under surveillance, with zero privacy, can lead to feeling disconnected from who you really are, forcing you to wear a facade to conceal your true thoughts and emotions.

Another deeply harmful aspect of living under such control is how it crushes critical thinking. By silencing differing opinions and punishing any deviation from the party line, authoritarian leaders promote a culture where everyone just falls in line. Ironically, while these leaders may brag about their nation's stability and unity, they're actually suffocating the variety of ideas that drive innovation and growth. In a society where questioning and exploring are frowned upon, progress comes to a halt, stuck in whatever future the rulers have decided is the only correct one.

For those enduring life under authoritarian regimes, finding resilience is key. It's about discovering ways to stay true to yourself despite the enormous pressure to fit in. Building and leaning on a network of support is vital in this scenario. Look for people or groups who understand what you're going through. Realizing you're not alone can massively counter the feelings of isolation and hopelessness that such systems generate.

Engage in activities that enhance your mental and emotional well-being. Whether it's art, reading, exercising, or meditation, actively seek ways to maintain your independence and inner peace. Utilize technology wisely to connect with allies while staying vigilant against potential surveillance risks. Utilizing tools that encrypt messages can offer a more secure means of communication without compromising your personal security. Educate yourself and raise awareness about the psychological impact of living under such stressful circumstances. Knowledge equips you to recognize stress and trauma symptoms in yourself and others, guiding you toward prioritizing your mental health.

Research from Boski et al. in 2015 shows that countries with a good balance of freedom and control have better mental and social outcomes. This means that communities do well when there's a mix of safety and personal freedom. It's vital to have both to avoid negative effects on people's minds. These findings underline the need for policies that protect personal freedoms, especially in places moving towards more controlling systems.

The Loss of Medical Bodily Autonomy

The covid-19 pandemic brought on a situation where governments around the world decided to make it mandatory for people to take vaccines quickly developed to combat the virus. Many people felt they were being forced to inject substances into their bodies without having enough time to properly test them. It made many uncomfortable and worried about their basic human rights.

During the pandemic, the government introduced mandates that pressured the citizens to get vaccinated under threat of financial and social consequences. Many feel that governments around the world aimed to remove the individual's basic human right to bodily autonomy with overreaching control. These mandates caused many individuals to feel uncertain about their rights. People who were hesitant about the vaccines found themselves in a tough spot, having to choose between their medical autonomy and aligning with the government's directives.

Apart from the government, corporations also played a role in pushing for vaccinations among their employees. Companies, in an attempt to control their employees while hiding behind the guise of government mandates, began requiring their staff to get vaccinated under threat of termination. The choice for employees seemed to be complying with the overreaching corporate rules or facing the risk of losing their jobs, their ability to feed their families, and their entire livelihood. This added pressure from the corporations heightened the tension among workers, leaving them to weigh the importance of their employment against their autonomy and their basic human rights.

The combined efforts of the government and corporations to enforce vaccination stirred fear and anxiety within the population. Employees felt a sense of coercion, fearing the repercussions of non-compliance. The strategy of using threats of termination to ensure vaccination compliance left employees feeling trapped and uncertain about their future. This approach led many individuals to question the extent to which their personal rights were being restricted during these unprecedented times.

As the mandates became more stringent, individuals began experiencing a growing unease and frustration. Many felt that their freedom of choice was being challenged, as they were being compelled to conform to unscientific vaccination requirements. The pressure to comply without questioning the mandates further fueled the sense of discontent and unrest among the population. The evolving circumstances during the pandemic created a shift in societal dynamics, with individuals grappling to navigate between personal autonomy and societal expectations.

The combined effect of these mandates and coercions during the pandemic had a significant impact on society as a whole. It created divisions among people, with some blindly following the directives while others resisted, leading to conflicts and tensions in various communities. This loss of trust in authorities and fear of repercussions had a profound effect on the way people viewed the concept of medical bodily autonomy.

Self-Care and Resilience in Oppressive Environments

Living under the grip of authoritarian regimes isn't just about losing freedom and civil rights; it deeply affects the mental health of its people. The continuous pressure and fear from such oppressive conditions can lead to ongoing psychological distress unless properly managed. Thankfully, there are methods people can adopt to lessen these effects and keep their mental health in check despite tough situations.

Stepping into this challenge requires building resilience through coping skills that help tackle everyday stress with strength. Practices like mindfulness have proven effective. They cultivate a moment-to-moment awareness that enables individuals to handle feelings of anxiety and despair more adeptly. Moreover, finding support within the community creates a sense of unity and shared purpose, very important in places where isolation and suspicion run high. By forming or joining informal networks and groups, one finds emotional backing and a chance for collaboration, reminding them they're not battling alone.

Turning to professional psychological support is another key step. Accessing counseling or therapy provides vital tools for dealing with stress, trauma, and anxiousness. Therapy offers a private space to work through emotions, helping someone build effective coping mechanisms. It's essential to view seeking assistance as an act of strength, breaking down any negative perceptions around mental health care.

Taking care of oneself is fundamentally important for mental well-being. Simple routines like regular exercise, good nutrition, and ample rest make a big difference. Keeping up social ties is crucial too. Staying connected with loved ones, even through digital means, fights off loneliness and provides emotional support. Being gentle with oneself through tough times is also necessary, as it builds endurance and helps avoid exhaustion.

Resilience against authoritarianism requires a comprehensive approach that combines self-awareness, learning, and connecting with others. Understanding your rights and how authoritarian regimes work equips you with the knowledge to confront challenges directly. Educational initiatives that foster critical thinking and promote civic participation empower individuals to contribute meaningfully to their communities, fostering a sense of empowerment. Engaging in community activities, such as volunteering, participating in local politics, or joining movements, builds collective resilience and counters the feelings of helplessness often imposed by authoritarian systems.

Brannen et al. (2020) stress the significance of fostering strategies to confront digital authoritarianism. They argue that resisting such threats involves bolstering democracy and human rights globally. This principle supports the wider goal of empowering those under autocratic control by nurturing resilience through informed involvement in democratic actions.

For mindfulness and community support, incorporate short mindfulness exercises into your daily routine and join groups or forums that match your interests or needs. Sharing your journey and strategies with peers can provide helpful perspectives and moral support. When considering therapy, choose therapists or services familiar with the challenges of living under such regimes. Opt for online therapy if meeting in person is risky due to surveillance or other restrictions. To maintain social connections, schedule regular times to connect with loved ones using secure communication tools. Hosting virtual gatherings can help strengthen relationships and offer mutual support. For building resilience through learning and engagement, find reliable news sources and educational materials that explain authoritarianism and ways to resist it. Participate in community-led workshops or online learning opportunities that focus on civic education, digital skills, and understanding your rights.

Long-Term Societal Implications of Psychological Trauma

Living under authoritarian rule has deep psychological effects and impacts society in complex ways. Over time, people living in such conditions often experience collective trauma, leading to the acceptance of oppression as normal and an increase in mistrust among community members. This situation affects not just those currently living, but also leaves a lasting imprint on future generations, challenging the unity and well-being of societies.

Experiencing collective trauma means that entire communities or nations feel psychological harm together, which goes beyond individual suffering. For example, after Stalinist regimes, areas in Eastern and Central Europe that faced higher death rates due to harsh policies showed a stronger resistance to authoritarian figures many years later. This suggests that such trauma can instill a deep distrust towards any political force reminiscent of past oppressors, as well as within society itself, showing how long-lasting these scars can be.

Healing from these deep psychological wounds requires more than just surface-level solutions. Efforts similar to the truth and reconciliation processes seen in Rwanda after the genocide are essential for rebuilding trust. These efforts encourage open discussions about past crimes and experiences, involving both victims and perpetrators. It's important, however, to adapt these healing methods to fit the unique historical and cultural contexts of each affected society. By incorporating local traditions and structures, initiatives can be more effective in achieving true reconciliation and recovery.

Additionally, creating a culture of empathy, understanding, and solidarity is vital in overcoming collective trauma. Programs like those in Rwanda, which bring together different parts of the community for guided conversations on safety, trust, and respect, can significantly aid in societal healing. These initiatives should aim to include everyone, especially those most impacted and marginalized, and integrate local cultural elements to help build connections and mutual understanding. Regularly assessing and adjusting these programs is also key to meeting the changing needs of the community.

Understanding the long-term effects of psychological trauma is vital for shaping public discussions and policies aimed at justice, accountability, and human rights protection. This commitment to advocacy is not only about addressing past wrongs but also preventing future oppression. Participating in discussions, supporting victim's rights groups, and contributing to memorials are practical ways for individuals and communities to engage in this effort. Educating younger generations about historical traumas and their ongoing effects can also equip them with the empathy and knowledge necessary to avoid repeating such events.

The process of healing and reconciliation in communities affected by authoritarianism is indeed complex and requires efforts from individuals, communities, and institutions alike. Rooted in empathy, understanding, and a dedication to justice and human rights, taking steps towards recovery involves adopting specific healing processes, promoting empathy, and standing up for accountability. Through this approach, societies can start healing from the wounds of collective trauma, moving towards a future that is inclusive, resilient, and kind.

It's clear that promoting critical thinking, fostering community bonds, and prioritizing self-care are important acts of defiance. These actions, though they may appear simple, have a profound impact on society at large, potentially changing its trajectory.

The mental burden that comes with living under authoritarian regimes has repercussions that reach far beyond individual suffering. It affects the very fabric of society, weakening its ability to withstand and rebound from future adversities. Therefore, it is vital for everyone involved - whether they are government officials, policymakers, activists, scholars, or everyday citizens - to not just comprehend these dynamics but to actively participate in creating spaces where freedom, independence, and mental health can thrive.

Chapter 9

Global Perspectives on Authoritarian Control

Across the world, leaders with authoritarian tendencies have skillfully tightened their hold on power using a wide range of methods that differ greatly from one area to another. This ability to adapt to the ever-evolving global landscape not only highlights their agility but also the intricate ways in which they exert control. They've become increasingly savvy, manipulating media and information, and even rigging electoral processes to ensure they stay in charge, showcasing an unexpected level of cleverness in keeping people under their rule.

One of the main issues with authoritarian regimes isn't merely their presence, but how they blend into various cultural and socio-political contexts so seamlessly, making them a particularly stubborn type of governance to shake off. Their knack for adapting is a big hurdle for anyone dedicated to safeguarding democratic principles. The sneaky techniques these regimes use to quell any opposition, along with their strategic twisting of laws and governing bodies, make it tough to pinpoint and oppose their tactics. Additionally, the way they harness technology and globalization adds more layers to this complex problem. Their influence connects across borders through international networks, raising the stakes when it comes to matters of global governance, security, and human rights.

Despite the daunting task, getting a handle on the varied ways authoritarianism rears its head globally sets the stage for crafting more effective countermeasures. By taking a close look at how authoritarian leaders operate and the consequences of their actions on civil liberties, governance, and global relations, this discussion aims to arm policymakers, activists, and the general populace with the insights necessary to challenge and diminish the reach of authoritarianism. The ultimate ambition is to catalyze a robust worldwide movement that staunchly defends democratic ideals and the protection of personal freedoms against the looming threat of tyranny.

Diverse Authoritarian Tactics and Strategies

When looking into the tactics and strategies authoritarian governments use around the world, it's fascinating to see how their methods of staying in power can be quite different. At the heart of understanding these differences is realizing that even though authoritarians might all want to concentrate power and quash dissent, the way they go about it changes depending on where you look.

For instance, controlling information and media is something many authoritarian regimes do, but how they do it can vary substantially. Some countries might go for heavy-handed censorship and owning most media outlets. However, as Sergei Guriev and Daniel Treisman pointed out in 2019, there's a trend towards more sneaky ways of shaping what the public sees and hears. This creates a false sense of openness while ensuring only the "right" kind of information gets out.

Elections under authoritarian rule offer another interesting point of discussion. You'd think having elections would lean towards democracy, but looking closer, it's clear they're often just for show. They're set up to make the government look legitimate without actually risking losing power. Tactics like election fraud or scaring off the opposition are common. This idea of 'competitive authoritarianism,' where elections happen but aren't fair, is getting more notice worldwide (Freedom House, 2022).

Authoritarian regimes have also proven themselves to be highly adaptable over time. They've been quick to take up new technologies for spying and are not shy about going after their critics, even beyond their borders. This shows how these governments evolve to face new challenges and keep their iron grip on power.

Then there's the concept of 'coup-proofing' – various tricks authoritarians use to stop coups before they happen. This might mean setting up rival military groups or sowing distrust within the armed forces. These methods highlight how insecure these leaders can feel about their power. Though these tactics might work in the short term, they come with big downsides, like less effective militaries and wasted resources.

Understanding all these different authoritarian tricks is very important for anyone wanting to support democracy and push back against tyranny. Knowing what authoritarians do - from manipulating information to undermining genuine democracy - helps activists, policymakers, and the international community to come up with better strategies in response. It's about actively engaging with these issues, rather than just acknowledging that they exist.

The reports by organizations like Freedom House in 2022 are key in shining a light on how authoritarianism is changing and spreading. They stress how important it is for democratic countries to stand together and support groups and institutions that resist authoritarian overreach.

The Freedom Convoy and The Authoritarian Response

The Canadian Convoy Protests of 2022, known as the 'Freedom Convoy', began in response to the COVID-19 Vaccine Mandates and restrictions in Canada. These protests emerged due to objections to vaccine mandates along the United States border but soon grew to include broader COVID-19 measures. It all started on January 22 when a substantial number of vehicles set forth from various regions, traveling across provinces. The convoys eventually converged in Ottawa on January 29, 2022, where participants gathered for a rally at Parliament Hill. Thousands of pedestrians also joined in to show their support for the cause.

The convoy protests provided a platform for individuals to voice their concerns about the vaccine mandates and COVID-19 restrictions. Participants came together to peacefully express their opposition to the government's policies, seeking to make their voices heard through peaceful demonstration. The gathering of numerous vehicles and people symbolized unity and solidarity among those who shared similar grievances. By coming together, they aimed to draw attention to their cause and bring about change through collective action.

The 'Freedom Convoy' sparked a national dialogue on issues surrounding vaccine mandates and COVID-19 restrictions. As the convoys made their way through various provinces, they garnered attention and initiated discussions among Canadians from all walks of life. The protests served as a focal point for debates on personal freedoms, bodily autonomy, public health measures, and government policies. This movement not only captured the public's interest but also prompted reflections on the balance between individual rights and public safety concerns during times of crisis.

The convoy protests symbolized unity and resistance against perceived infringements on personal liberties and freedoms. Participants viewed the movement as a way to stand together in opposition to what they deemed as overreaching government mandates. The convoy's journey across provinces signified a collective effort to push back against measures that many felt were limiting their autonomy. By converging in Ottawa, participants aimed to send a powerful message of solidarity and defiance against policies they believed were unjust.

What began as a response to vaccine mandates at the United States border soon resonated on a national scale. The 'Freedom Convoy' drew attention not only in Canada but also internationally, making headlines and sparking conversations about civil liberties and public health strategies. The movement's significance extended beyond its initial scope, highlighting global concerns regarding individual rights, government intervention, and societal responses to public health crises. The convoy protests underscored the interconnectedness of issues across borders and the power of grassroots movements in shaping public discourse.

The convoy protests empowered community participation and activism among individuals who felt marginalized or unheard. By joining the convoys or showing support in various ways, people had the opportunity to engage in civic action and express their viewpoints on critical social issues. The movement encouraged diverse voices to come together and advocate for change through peaceful means. Through their involvement, participants demonstrated their commitment to civic engagement and their determination to influence policy decisions that affected their lives.

The rallies at Parliament Hill symbolized a collective call for change and a demand for greater transparency and accountability from governing bodies. Participants gathered to make their voices heard, calling for a reevaluation of current policies and a more inclusive decision-making process. The gatherings served as a platform for individuals to share their stories, concerns, and hopes for a better future. By uniting in a common cause, participants sought to bring about tangible changes that reflected the will and needs of the people.

The convoy protests prompted a moment of reflection on the power of grassroots movements and the role of peaceful protests in effecting social change. The gatherings underscored the significance of community-driven initiatives in shaping public discourse and influencing policy outcomes.

Participants and supporters alike took stock of the impact of their actions and the potential for collective movements to bring about meaningful transformations in society. The 'Freedom Convoy' served as a reminder of the potency of organized action and the enduring spirit of democratic participation.

Democratic Rights vs. Authoritarian Response

While Canada is recognized as a democracy where citizens have the right to peaceful protest and voice discontent, the government, under Prime Minister Justin Trudeau's leadership, responded to the protests utilizing what many viewed as authoritarian strategies.

These protests in Canada have gained worldwide attention due to the way the government dealt with them. People's participation in these protests was met with responses that many perceived as authoritarian. The government's actions were heavily criticized, and many considered them to be using excessive force. This led to a debate on the balance between security measures and respecting citizens' rights to protest.

Several actions by government officials were deemed illegal, including vandalizing protesters' vehicles, and unlawfully confiscating their fuel. These actions were seen as aggressive and unnecessary, and it raised concerns about the use of force against peaceful demonstrators. It was clear to many that these actions taken by the government were just methods to limit the protesters' resources and hinder their ability to continue their demonstration.

Another concerning action during the protests was the obstruction of supporters who were trying to provide essential supplies such as financial support, food, and water to those involved in the demonstrations. Preventing the provision of necessities to the protesters raised ethical questions about the government's handling of the situation. This obstruction was viewed as a violation of the protesters' rights and sparked conversations about the government's responsibility to ensure the safety and well-being of its citizens, even during protests.

Prime Minister Trudeau took drastic measures by freezing and seizing the bank accounts of donors supporting the protesters without valid legal grounds. This step was part of implementing the Canadian War Times Act, which mirrored the enforcement seen in martial law in the United States. Trudeau's handling of the situation, alongside his refusal to engage in dialogue with the protesters, raised concerns about his approach resembling that of a tyrannical dictator, rather than a democratically elected leader.

The government's response to the protests sparked various discussions regarding the limits of power in a democracy. The use of what many people around the globe considered authoritarian tactics triggered debates about the role of the government in ensuring public safety while respecting individuals' rights to express their opinions. These events highlighted the need for transparency and accountability in government actions, especially when dealing with protests.

The protests in Canada and the government's response prompted reflections on the delicate balance between maintaining order and upholding democratic values. As we continue to navigate these challenges, it is essential to engage in constructive dialogue, uphold the principles of democracy, and address the concerns raised by citizens. The events surrounding the protests served as a reminder of the importance of respecting people's rights while ensuring public safety and order.

The World Economic Forum

The World Economic Forum, established by Klaus Schwab, brings together a collective of the world's most wealthy individuals who utilize their abundant financial resources to shape national governments and establish worldwide regulations, all without any democratic approval from the public. Impacts of their decisions are felt across various aspects of society, yet the average citizen has no say in selecting or holding these billionaires accountable for their policy-making influence.

Klaus Schwab, the founder of the World Economic Forum, stands at the helm of this organization, steering its members towards significant power plays in the global political arena. Through their substantial wealth, these billionaires wield an unmatched level of authority, exerting their influence over governments far and wide without direct accountability to the people.

A striking claim made by Klaus Schwab himself is the infiltration of governments by the Forum's young global leaders. This statement hints at a covert operation wherein selected individuals work their way into the decision-making bodies of various countries, implementing policies that reflect the interests of the Forum's wealthy elite.

The policies crafted by the World Economic Forum hold remarkable sway over international affairs, despite the absence of any democratic input from the citizens affected by these decisions. Such policies can dictate economic directions, environmental actions, and even social reforms, yet the general public remains disconnected from the process.

One of the key areas where the Forum exerts its influence is in shaping economic policies that have ramifications on a global scale. From trade regulations to investment strategies, these decisions can impact the financial well-being of nations and individuals alike, all orchestrated by a select group of billionaires with absolutely no direct accountability.

Environmental policies, vital for the future of the planet, also fall under the purview of the World Economic Forum. The decisions made regarding sustainability, environmental protection, and resource management are steered by individuals who may not have the ecological well-being of the Earth as their top priority, raising questions about the true intentions behind such policies.

Social reforms and initiatives that affect communities and individuals often bear the imprint of the Forum's influence. From education systems to healthcare structures, the policies recommended and implemented by these wealthy individuals can reshape entire societies, all without the consent or involvement of those directly impacted by these changes.

The World Economic Forum, under the leadership of Klaus Schwab, operates as a powerful entity, molding global policies and decisions with far-reaching consequences. The lack of democratic oversight in the actions taken by this organization raises concerns about the tyrannical nature of their influence and the implications for the citizens of democratic nations worldwide.

Cultural and Historical Factors Influencing Authoritarianism

Exploring how culture and history shape attitudes towards authoritarian governance reveals the deep-seated impact of these factors on societal views. This investigation brings to light the intricate role cultural norms have in making some groups more inclined towards authoritarian regimes. The intertwined nature of historical events with cultural practices adds layers to understanding why certain communities might lean towards such governance systems.

When we look into cultural norms, we uncover a complex network of beliefs, traditions, and values that organize and influence everyday life. These norms are often rooted in long-standing traditions and shared experiences, crafting the community's perspective of the world. In environments where respect for authority and hierarchical structures are ingrained, authoritarian governments tend to thrive. The natural alignment between these cultural practices and authoritarian governance means that, in many instances, this governance style is not just tolerated but even preferred due to its resonance with local values of order, stability, and strong leadership.

Historical contexts also play a crucial role in shaping societies' tilt towards authoritarianism. Delving into historical accounts allows us to trace back the origins of authoritarian inclinations within different cultures. For example, "The Global Expansion of Authoritarian Rule" (House, 2022) provides insight into how historical turmoil and the desire for stability have influenced political leanings across generations. This emphasizes the importance of understanding history to comprehend current political tendencies, including the persistence or emergence of authoritarian regimes.

Furthermore, the significance of social values in shaping political landscapes is undeniable. These values, which dictate what a society deems important or right, directly sway political preferences. In places where there's a high value placed on conformity, tradition, and communal harmony over individual rights, authoritarianism finds a more welcoming environment. This reveals the profound effect of societal values on the type of governance that gains acceptance.

The connection between culture and history helps us understand why some people accept authoritarian leaders. By studying this link, we can learn how to resist authoritarianism. It shows that the stories we tell about our culture and history can change. This change can create opportunities for democracy to grow. Sharing stories of empowerment and getting involved in community activities can weaken support for authoritarian leaders.

Recognizing the influence of culture and history is vital for anyone advocating for democracy. By understanding the roots of authoritarian acceptance, tailor-made strategies that align with the specific cultural and historical backdrop of a society can be developed. Emphasizing universal aspirations for dignity and freedom while acknowledging cultural particulars presents a strategy for fostering democratic values in places previously swayed by authoritarian tendencies.

International Alliances Against Authoritarian Influence

Understanding the importance of working with other countries to resist authoritarian control is like peeling an onion. Each layer we remove reveals more complexity that we need to pay attention to. Looking back at past actions against authoritarian rule helps us learn which strategies to use now and which ones to avoid, since the basic principles of authoritarianism tend to remain the same over time.

As we dig deeper into this topic, we encounter the complex network of global power relations. It's key to understand that countries don't operate in a vacuum; their interrelations are influenced by various factors such as economic ties, security issues, and geopolitical tactics. Grasping this web of interactions is crucial for nations to work together effectively against authoritarian threats. It's akin to organizing a group project where every participant brings a unique background to the table; understanding everyone's strengths and limitations is essential for success.

When we look at successful examples of international cooperation, we see the power of collective action in fostering democracy. The concerted global reaction to apartheid in South Africa, or the more recent international sanctions aimed at regimes violating human rights, highlight how united action based on common values can tackle even the toughest challenges. However, it goes beyond mere sanctions or military interventions; it's equally about bolstering civil societies, advocating for human rights, and ensuring aid meets the real needs of local communities.

On the flip side, scrutinizing the impediments and hurdles of international interventions helps shape realistic strategies to fight authoritarianism. Not all efforts lead to success, and some might have unintended downsides that make things worse. Learning from these outcomes enables the development of flexible and nuanced plans, tailored to specific situations. It also stresses the importance of favoring diplomatic paths and boosting local capabilities first and foremost.

Working together internationally is vital in reducing the influence of authoritarian leaders. These leaders benefit from causing division by using tactics like spreading false information to create disagreements among democracies. By standing together, strongly committing to democratic values, and collaborating across borders, we can effectively oppose authoritarian expansion. This emphasizes that the pursuit of democracy is not confined to one country but requires a joint effort on a global scale with unified determination and action.

Considering this, we see that while there are no simple solutions, there exists a route highlighted by teamwork, learning, and flexibility. Addressing authoritarianism demands patience, determination, and steadfast support for democratic systems and principles. This entails combining resources, exchanging knowledge, and coordinating policies in a way that respects national sovereignty while embracing global standards for human rights and governance.

This discussion invites each of us to reflect on how we can contribute to this collective endeavor. From staying well-informed and advocating for sound foreign policy to supporting groups actively working towards democracy, everyone has a part to play. It emphasizes that democracy is an ongoing process needing continuous care, vigilance, and active participation rather than a final goal.

In exploring these topics, maintaining discussions rooted in factual evidence and led by empathy is essential. Recognizing the human ramifications of authoritarian regimes—the suppression of free speech, erosion of liberties, and silencing of critics—necessitates a response driven by a shared humanity and a universal yearning for dignity, respect, and autonomy. With this perspective, the engagement of international alliances and interventions in opposing authoritarianism transcends strategic necessity; it becomes a moral obligation.

Interconnectedness of Authoritarian Regimes

In today's world, it has become increasingly clear that authoritarian governments are getting quite good at expanding their influence beyond their own countries. They use complex networks that go beyond geographical and ideological differences to create a sort of global web that affects us all. This situation highlights how important it is for democracies to work together more closely to address this challenge because when one authoritarian state makes a move, it can have ripple effects worldwide, impacting many other countries.

Taking a closer look into how these regimes operate in the digital world gives us valuable insights. A study by Fell (2024) sheds light on how these governments strategically take control over key parts of the internet to extend their influence. They manage the infrastructure that helps data travel across the globe, not just within their own borders but also extending their reach to support less powerful allies with technology gifts. This approach underlines the modern reality where digital pathways become tools for spreading authoritarian control.

The consequences of such cyber tactics reveal how deeply connected authoritarian countries are, through a mix of economic, political, and social ties. When wealthier autocracies provide technological assistance to poorer ones, it creates a network that promotes authoritarian values, affecting governance and information freedom on a global scale. This situation highlights the complexity of international power dynamics and shows how these actions challenge global norms around openness and accountability.

To counter this, understanding the cooperation between authoritarian regimes is crucial. It reveals potential weaknesses in their alliances and strategies that democratic nations can exploit. For example, improving internet architecture through decentralized systems like Internet Exchange Points (IXPs) reduces dependence on networks controlled by authoritarians. This strategy could help maintain a freer internet less prone to manipulation by these regimes.

Additionally, examining how these states intertwine economically, politically, and socially offers insights into their global influence. The export of censorship technology and surveillance methods is particularly alarming, as it represents an effort to spread authoritarian principles worldwide. This global network of influence calls for a unified and strong response from democratic countries to protect our fundamental freedoms and principles.

Understanding the extent of authoritarian connections globally helps in crafting defenses for democracy. Acknowledging the broad reach of these influences allows democracies to formulate comprehensive strategies. This includes enhancing cybersecurity, protecting information integrity, and forming coalitions to uphold democratic standards.

Recognizing the collaborative nature of authoritarian regimes is vital for developing effective counter-strategies. By pooling resources, sharing intelligence, and adopting best practices, democracies can strengthen their position against authoritarian intrusion. Essentially, this involves creating a secure digital environment that upholds values such as freedom and privacy.

Addressing the challenge posed by authoritarianism requires a detailed grasp of its global impact. Tackling these issues collectively, rather than in isolation, is essential for success. In today's interconnected world, democratic countries need to collaborate more closely to face the assertive nature of authoritarian states head-on. By combining their capabilities and dedicating themselves to democratic governance, they can build a safer, more prosperous world.

Authoritarian regimes are a big problem for democracies worldwide. This complicated situation puts freedoms in danger. People who care about democracy and protecting individual rights, like government officials, activists, or researchers, learn important things from these discussions. These lessons are a strong call to take action. Ignoring the rise of authoritarianism is risky because it could lead to losing personal freedoms and even damage democratic governance globally.

Chapter 10

Towards a Future of Freedom and Democracy

Protecting our rights and the foundations of democracy is vital as we face an ever-evolving political environment. The increase in digital data gathering and surveillance puts our personal privacy and freedom at risk. When personal information is misused, it can deeply affect our democratic systems, underlining the critical need for strong regulations on data privacy. As we explore these issues further, it's evident that safeguarding democratic values involves more than just watching from the sidelines; it requires active engagement and a solid plan to ensure every citizen's rights are preserved.

The fading trust in governmental actions and the reduced clarity in how decisions are made present real dangers to the stability of democratic institutions. Around the globe, respect for the rule of law is weakening, and judicial systems are becoming more influenced by political agendas, jeopardizing the essence of equitable governance. This lack of openness and responsibility decreases public faith and makes it difficult for people to call their leaders into account. The autonomy of courts, crucial to democracy, is under attack by those aiming to amass power, underscoring the importance of establishing measures to prevent unfairness and guarantee legal fairness for all.

Safeguarding Civil Liberties and Democratic Institutions

In our journey to uphold democratic values and safeguard personal freedoms, it's important that we give top priority to protecting civil liberties and democratic frameworks. A closer look at this challenge points us toward several key actions worth taking a deep dive into.

A critical first step is bringing in strong data privacy regulations. Nowadays, when collecting someone's personal information has become all too easy and its misuse all too common, setting up strong protections for this data is very important. These laws act as a fortress, keeping our private information safe from being misused. To get this right, we need to kickstart comprehensive laws that spell out what counts as personal data and lay down rules on how it can be collected, used, and shared. We must also put tough penalties in place to deter anyone, be it government or companies, from mishandling personal information, and make sure there's complete openness about how data is handled, giving people control over their own information, including the right to fix or remove it.

Next up, making sure that government actions are transparent is vital for building trust and accountability in our democratic systems. This relies on the idea that when people have the right information, they can hold their leaders to account. To make transparency work well, we should require that government activities, decisions, and policies are regularly made public in formats everyone can understand. We should set up independent watchdogs to keep an eye on and report how transparent the government is being. We must foster a culture of public involvement by inviting feedback and participation in important discussions and decision-making processes.

Legal principles are the foundation of a fair society. One essential aspect is maintaining the rule of law, which ensures that all individuals, regardless of their status, abides by the same legal standards.. Nobody should be above the law, and there shouldn't be special rules based on who you are. For this to work effectively, it involves making sure that people in power don't misuse their authority. One key way to do this is by protecting the independence of the judicial system. This means the courts and judges should be able to make decisions without being influenced by politicians, the super wealthy, or others in power.

It's essential to protect the independence of the judiciary. This means judges should be able to make rulings based on the law and the facts of the case rather than outside pressures. To achieve this, practical steps need to be taken.

For example, legal reforms can be put in place to prevent political interference in judicial decisions. When judges can work independently, it helps ensure that justice is served fairly and impartially.

Another vital aspect is to make legal concepts more accessible to the public. Understanding how the legal system works can help people have more confidence in it. Educating the public about their legal rights and responsibilities can also create a more just society. One way to do this is by offering legal education programs that explain basic legal concepts in simple language. When people understand the law better, they are more likely to respect it and follow it.

To maintain the integrity of the judicial system, it's essential to have robust procedures in place for selecting, evaluating, and disciplining judges. When judges are chosen based on their qualifications and ability to interpret the law effectively, it strengthens the legal system. Evaluating judges regularly can ensure that they continue to meet the required standards of competency and integrity. Disciplinary measures should be in place to address any misconduct promptly.

In selecting judges, the focus should be on their competency, integrity, and merit. These qualities are vital for upholding the rule of law. By prioritizing these factors over superficial criteria such as race or gender, the judicial system can maintain its credibility. Judges who possess the necessary skills and ethical standards are more likely to make sound judgments that uphold justice.

To give one example: In 2022, Judge Ketanji Brown Jackson was nominated to the Supreme Court by President Joe Biden. Later that year, following confirmation by the U.S. Senate, she took her oath of office. Judge Jackson, who was celebrated for being a trailblazing *woman*, refused to provide any sort of definition of the word 'woman'. In a noteworthy exchange with Sen. Marsha Blackburn of Tennessee, inquiring about the definition of 'woman,' Judge Jackson, stating her judicial role is to "resolve disputes", asserted that the reason she cannot define the word 'woman' is because she is "not a biologist". This reluctance to define a fundamental term raises concerns about her ability to impartially interpret laws affecting American women. How can one effectively uphold the rights of all citizens, particularly women, if there exists uncertainty surrounding the definition of a woman?

Upholding the rule of law and safeguarding the independence of the judiciary are fundamental to a just society. By strengthening the autonomy of the judiciary, enhancing public understanding of legal principles, and prioritizing competency and integrity in the selection of judges, we can ensure that the legal system remains fair and impartial for all.

Furthermore, getting the public actively involved in creating policies is essential for a thriving democracy. When citizens play a part in crafting laws and policies, the results are more likely to reflect a wide range of societal views and better protect everyone's freedoms. We can encourage active public participation by making it simpler for people from all walks of life to take part in consultations, using technology to open up more channels for people to contribute from afar, and teaching people how to effectively participate in these processes, ensuring they're well-equipped to make meaningful contributions.

Policy recommendations from sources like Freedom House highlight the importance of such steps. Their research supports the view that these efforts would not only defend individual rights but also strengthen democratic institutions against weakening. They call for changes that go beyond just passing new laws, embedding the principles of openness, legal fairness, and citizen involvement into the very essence of governance.

It's also vital to remember that while these guidelines point us in the right direction, realizing them requires ongoing dedication and the readiness to adapt. As society changes, our methods for defending democracy must evolve too. This continuous process needs our alertness, creativity, and commitment to always getting better.

The involvement of policymakers and the collective voice of individuals is invaluable in this regard. Through collaboration, embracing new ideas, and fostering an environment where different viewpoints are respected, we can tackle the complexities of modern-day governance. It's all about creating an environment where conversations thrive, differences of opinion are valued, and diverse perspectives come together in pursuit of shared objectives.

This method reflects a broader ambition to cultivate a democratic society that respects its core values while staying open to change. It strikes a balance between security and freedom, leadership and empowerment, tradition and innovation. These efforts lay the groundwork for a durable democratic system capable of resisting internal and external threats to its integrity.

The Importance of Civic Engagement and Political Participation

Getting involved in civic activities and playing an active role in politics are vital for a robust democracy. They ensure that our society mirrors the various needs and voices of its people. Being part of the democratic process is more than a privilege; it's a significant duty that supports our cherished values and helps society move forward. For our democracy to thrive, it's very important that citizens actively participate. This not only strengthens our institutions against threats of tyranny, but also enriches public debates and makes our government more accountable.

Understanding the intricate issues of today's political landscape requires us to stay well-informed. This means we need to do more than just watch the news. We should critically assess the information we receive, question where it comes from, and talk about it with others. This interaction helps sharpen our perspectives. Develop a habit of looking at different news outlets to make sure you're getting a variety of viewpoints. Try to engage with discussions in your community or online to hear different opinions. Always encourage open-minded and respectful conversations among friends and family to foster a learning environment.

It's equally important to engage in local movements, protests, and advocacy efforts to defend democracy. These activities empower us to demand change, hold leaders accountable, and ensure our government prioritizes the well-being of its people. To contribute significantly, identify causes that align with your beliefs and thoroughly educate yourself about them. Connect with local or online groups that host events and campaigns focusing on these issues. Offer your skills in organizing, digital communication, or legal expertise to support these causes. Participate in peaceful protests and respectful advocacy as effective methods to drive change.

Moreover, creating strong bonds within your community encourages collective action, helping everyone come together to face challenges. This solidarity is imperative in counteracting the divide-and-conquer tactics often employed by authoritarian regimes. You can strengthen your community ties by organizing or participating in local events that encourage support and unity, making spaces for everyone to discuss community matters, ensuring every voice is heard, and supporting local initiatives and businesses that aim to improve community life.

Backing diverse civil society organizations and fostering inclusive conversations is key to promoting a culture of civic involvement. These organizations play a major role in mobilizing resources, spreading awareness, and campaigning for changes in various domains, from human rights to environmental protection. They also act as mediators between the government and its people, facilitating essential dialogue for democratic governance. To engage with these organizations effectively, look into groups that match your interests and evaluate their impact, and attend forums and discussions they organize to deepen your understanding of social and political issues.

These actions underscore the idea that being civically engaged isn't just a one-off task; it's a lifestyle choice that nurtures our democracy over time. As highlighted by the Center for Information & Research on Civic Learning and Engagement (CIRCLE, n.d.), starting these habits early sets the stage for a lifetime of active participation, leading to a fairer and more just society.

Engaging in civic activities has more benefits than just affecting policies and governance. It can lead to better academic performance, improve job opportunities, and increase well-being for those participating. Being actively involved also helps build social connections, creating a strong community bond and making neighborhoods healthier and more vibrant.

Addressing the disparities and obstacles that limit full civic participation is paramount. Efforts must focus on removing these barriers and crafting inclusive spaces that honor and incorporate every voice. Such an approach not only tackles representation and fairness issues but also reinforces the foundations of our democratic system.

Leveraging Technology for Democratic Governance

Harnessing the power of digital tools and platforms offers a fantastic chance to enhance trust and legitimacy in how democracies work. The heart of the matter goes beyond merely sharing data; it's about making it easy for citizens to find and understand this information, seeing clearly how their government makes decisions. This involves creating websites that are easy to use, providing up-to-the-minute updates on laws being passed, how money is being spent, and changes in policies. It's crucial that everyone can access these sites, including people with disabilities, and that they're available in different languages to reflect our diverse society.

How can we make sure these digital spaces truly benefit the public and encourage participation? Strategies to achieve this include keeping these platforms updated with the latest documents, decisions, and relevant data. Establishing clear standards for information sharing online to ensure consistency, reliability, and simplicity. Enhancing security measures to guard against cyber threats and uphold the integrity and accessibility of information. Advocating for educational programs that empower citizens to effectively navigate these tools and translate data into meaningful actions.

Beyond just looking at the data, introducing ways for open data exchange and gathering citizen feedback is key to making governments more responsive. This shift from simply consuming information to actively engaging in dialogue can forge stronger connections between governments and their citizens, ensuring decisions mirror what the public wants. Imagine having online forums for discussing policy, apps for giving feedback on city services, and even digital voting for community matters.

For this interactive approach to succeed, we must outline the aims and goals of open data projects to match what citizens need and what the government seeks to achieve. We must also craft a detailed plan for collecting, analyzing, and acting on feedback, making sure it truly shapes policymaking. Governments must be transparent about how citizen input is used, keeping the public informed about how their suggestions have led to action, reinforcing trust.

Tech has become vital in safeguarding democratic values. Utilizing digital tools can enhance oversight in elections and the battle against corruption. By monitoring campaign finances, ensuring fairness in elections, and facilitating quick reporting of electoral issues, these technologies have the potential to significantly reduce fraud and corruption. Through the use of blockchain technology for secure and transparent voting processes, creating detailed public records of campaign finances for scrutiny, as well as employing AI and data analysis to detect corrupt practices and election fraud early on, swift action can be taken.

The last element in empowering citizens revolves around digital literacy and promoting civic technology initiatives. Simply having access to tools isn't enough; understanding how to use them effectively is critical. Campaigns aimed at digital literacy can teach the public how to assess information online critically, engage digitally in societal matters, and know their digital rights and duties. Civic tech projects can also get the community involved in tackling local challenges, nurturing a spirit of innovation and collective responsibility for the community's wellbeing.

Consider collaborating with schools, charities, and tech firms to introduce educational programs centered on using technology in civic engagement. Support grassroots initiatives that bring tech solutions to local issues by providing financial aid, guidance, and technical resources. Establish a network among civic tech enthusiasts to share ideas, collaborate on projects, and drive innovation.

Fostering International Cooperation for Global Democracy

Building connections and partnerships between countries that cherish democracy is vital in today's world, where the push from authoritarian regimes challenges the very core of democratic ideals. Imagine countries working together like neighbors keeping an eye out for each other, but on a much larger scale. Each nation contributes its strengths—be it economic power, technological progress, or strong diplomatic ties—to form a powerful alliance aimed at defending freedom and dignity everywhere.

To enhance these alliances, we could establish regular meetings dedicated to discussions on democracy and human rights. These gatherings would serve as platforms for sharing intelligence and effective strategies among the allied nations. Additionally, organizing joint military exercises and creating defense agreements could serve as deterrents against authoritarian aggression. Starting a fund to support movements and independent media that advocate for democracy in authoritarian regimes would also make a strong statement about our unified stance for freedom.

Supporting global organizations and treaties that promote democracy and human rights is like setting the rules of a game and then making sure everyone sticks to them. But it's not enough to just talk the talk; financial backing, active involvement in decision-making, and adhering to established standards are necessary steps to make a tangible impact. This ensures that the principles we value are actively promoted and protected worldwide.

Focusing on strengthening institutions like the International Criminal Court and supporting key treaties will demonstrate our commitment to upholding democratic governance and human rights globally. Participating in peer reviews and supporting accountability measures within these frameworks encourages constant improvement among all involved, fortifying the legal structures essential for democracy.

Strategic engagement in aid programs that emphasize democratic governance is vital for helping nations face authoritarian threats. Such efforts should concentrate on building resilient institutions and public trust. By enhancing the capacity of local civil society, supporting free media, and bolstering fair electoral practices, we can help safeguard against undue influence. Educational programs fostering democratic values and critical thinking skills are essential for preparing future generations to contribute meaningfully to democratic society.

A customized approach is key when supporting democracies at risk, taking into account each country's unique situation. Diplomatic actions should aim to isolate governments that trample on human rights, using sanctions wisely but always leaving room for dialogue. Offering authoritarian leaders a way back into the international fold through improvements in governance and human rights acknowledges the potential for change.

Encouraging a worldwide embrace of democratic values involves sharing knowledge and experiences across borders, akin to knitting a vast fabric where every thread strengthens the weave of democracy. Programs like student exchanges, professional development, and cultural initiatives enrich understanding and solidarity among citizens of different countries. These efforts create a community eager to defend democracy and human rights on a global scale.

Moreover, showing support for activists fighting for these causes in oppressive environments is paramount. Recognizing their efforts with awards and public acknowledgment not only brings attention to their struggles but can also offer some protection from governmental backlash. The international reaction to the unfair treatment of dissidents often pressures authoritarian rulers to reconsider their actions, showcasing the impact of global unity.

Through unified efforts and deliberate measures, maintaining core democratic values is achievable. However, achieving this goal requires ongoing dedication and flexibility from both leaders and the community. This conversation should strike a chord with government officials, advocates, scholars, and engaged citizens alike, positioning them as key players in upholding the essence of democracy. The wider impact of our dialogue goes beyond just tweaking policies; it's about weaving democratic ideals into the very essence of how governments and societies operate daily.

Conclusion

The Dawn of a New Despotism: Understanding the Global Rise of Authoritarianism

Over the past few years, we've seen a significant shift in the global political landscape, with more countries leaning toward authoritarian rule. This shift is troubling, moving away from the democratic principles of freedom and equality that are at the core of many societies. The Freedom House's 2022 report highlights this concerning trend, showing an uptick in nations adopting government styles that concentrate power among the few, often sacrificing civil liberties and individual freedoms in the process. The consequences of this change are vast, affecting everything from how we talk about politics to our personal privacy.

The increase in authoritarianism is not just a political shift; it's a complex problem that poses a serious threat to democracy itself. It manifests in different ways, like spreading misinformation, ramping up surveillance, and weakening the checks and balances vital for democracy. These tactics don't just silence critics; they undermine trust in institutions, making it easier for governments to strengthen their grip on power without being held accountable. The speed at which this is happening worldwide sparks concern about how robust our democratic institutions are and what can be done to protect them from such threats. This issue goes beyond national boundaries, impacting global democracy and putting international cooperation and unity at risk.

To tackle this worrying trend, a comprehensive strategy is needed—one that encourages transparency, boosts accountability, and promotes civic education. We must look into effective ways to counter the rise of authoritarianism. By getting to grips with the methods and strategies authoritarian governments use, individuals and communities can better prepare themselves to push back against these forces. We've discussed concrete actions that governments, policymakers, activists, and everyday people can take to uphold democratic values. Through joint efforts and increased vigilance, there's a chance to reverse the authoritarian tide and strengthen democratic foundations across the globe.

Understanding the tactics used by authoritarian regimes equips us with the knowledge to defend against them. We must aim to dissect these strategies, offering insights into how information manipulation, surveillance expansion, and the undermining of democratic checks and balances occur. Recognizing these tactics enlightens us on the importance of safeguarding the principles that keep democratic systems resilient against such invasive measures. It's imperative for maintaining the integrity of our political discourse and ensuring that power remains a tool for public good, not for the consolidation of control.

Empowering citizens plays a key role in resisting authoritarian tendencies. Promoting awareness and understanding among the populace about their rights and the importance of democratic values lies at the heart of preserving liberty and equality. Educating people on how to critically assess information, engage in constructive political debate, and actively participate in governance processes fortifies the societal fabric against authoritarian encroachments. It's about fostering a culture that values transparency and holds leaders accountable, creating a more informed and engaged citizenry capable of standing up to threats against democracy.

In the fight against authoritarianism, collaboration is indispensable. It involves governments, policy makers, activists, and citizens coming together with a common goal: to defend democratic ideals and promote a fair, equal society. This collaborative approach underscores the necessity of collective action in identifying and implementing solutions that protect individual freedoms and civil liberties. By pooling resources, sharing knowledge, and coordinating efforts, stakeholders can create a united front against authoritarian advances, showcasing the power of solidarity in upholding democratic principles.

The Assault on Democracy and Privacy

Lately, we've seen a concerning shift worldwide from democratic practices to authoritarian rule. This change affects not just politics but the fabric of society itself, threatening values like freedom, equality, and mutual responsibility we cherish deeply. In the name of national security or public health, some governments have crossed lines they shouldn't have, compromising people's freedoms and privacy along the way.

One notable instance is outlined in Freedom House's 2022 report, which shows how authoritarian governments are getting better at sidestepping democratic norms and institutions. They're not only strengthening their grip on power within their own nations but also lending a hand to like-minded regimes, sparking a chain reaction that puts global democracy at risk. Alarmingly, 38% of people around the globe now live under 'Not Free' conditions, marking a high point not seen since 1997. This fact alone should alert us to the importance of defending democratic principles and the liberties they protect.

The challenge before us is complex. Authoritarian rulers use technology and social media for surveillance, to quell opposition, and to twist information to maintain their control. The collaboration of states with major tech firms further complicates matters, raising alarms over information monopoly and the degradation of public conversation. These alliances might boost economic growth initially but often do so at the expense of the common good, sidelining individual rights and privacy.

Facing these dangers, sitting back isn't an option. To preserve our democratic ideals and freedoms, it's essential for us all to resist collectively and take proactive steps. But what does this entail? Consider these actions:

- Push for more openness and accountability in dealings by both governments and companies, ensuring they prioritize the public good.
- Champion policies and technologies that safeguard personal privacy and data against unauthorized access and misuse.
- Get involved in educational efforts to spread the word about democracy's value and how to defend it from authoritarian tactics.
- Foster dialogue and cooperation among democracies to confront and curb authoritarianism's spread worldwide.

It's very important to realize the strength in our collective voice and actions. History is replete with instances of people uniting to defy oppression and push for progress. Staying informed, participating in our communities, and demanding accountability from leaders can direct our societies toward a future where freedom and democracy thrive.

This struggle against the encroachment of authoritarianism isn't merely about preserving our current lifestyle. It's about molding a society that prioritizes human well-being over unrestrained economic expansion, aiming for a balance between wealth, fairness, justice, and respect for individual rights. Given all of the compelling evidence, recognizing the gravity of our situation is critical.

We stand at a pivotal juncture, challenged to uphold our democratic values. However, I remain hopeful. Time and again, humanity has demonstrated remarkable resilience when facing trials. By drawing on shared strengths—our empathy, quest for justice, and firm dedication to liberty—we can counter the authoritarian forces seeking to undermine and divide us.

A Glimmer of Hope Amidst Rising Shadows

In exploring the shift from democratic values toward authoritarian rule, we've underscored the significant impact this trend has on both democracy itself and the individual freedoms we cherish. From the outset, we identified the growing infringement on these liberties as a pressing issue of our era. This examination reveals that the strength of democracy relies not solely on formal structures but also heavily on the commitment and efforts of people and communities around the globe.

Addressing this challenge requires a shared effort. Some critical actions we must take are, calling for increased transparency, advocating for privacy rights, participating in civic education, and encouraging global conversations. These strategies are not abstract ideas but rather tangible steps reflecting our collective duty to protect the democratic values that form the foundation of our societies.

Ignoring this call to action carries severe consequences, impacting not only our current state of well-being but also determining the heritage we pass on to the next generations. It paints a picture of a dystopian future where the vibrant tapestry of freedom and diversity is overshadowed by a monotonous landscape of global Tyranny.

References

- Carnegie Endowment for International Peace. (2024). *Denying Support for Chinese and China-Enabled Authoritarianism and Repression - U.S.-China Technological "Decoupling": A Strategy and Policy Framework.* [Webpage]. Retrieved from https://carnegieendowment.org/2022/04/25/denying-support-for-chinese-and-china-enabled-authoritarianism-and-repression-pub-86924

- Freedom House. (2022). *Countering an authoritarian overhaul of the internet.* Freedom House. Retrieved from https://freedomhouse.org/report/freedom-net/2022/countering-authoritarian-overhaul-internet

- Freedom House. (2023). *The repressive power of artificial intelligence.* Retrieved from https://freedomhouse.org/report/freedom-net/2023/repressive-power-artificial-intelligence

- Hinckley, R. A., & Harell, A. (2020). *Selective exposure and the authoritarian dynamic: Evidence from Canada and the United States. Journal of Social and Political Psychology,* 8(1), 151-172. https://doi.org/10.5964/jspp.v8i1.1085

- Osborne, D., Costello, T. H., Duckitt, J., & Sibley, C. G. (2023). *The psychological causes and societal consequences of authoritarianism. Nature Reviews Psychology*, 4(2), 220. https://doi.org/10.1038/s44159-023-00161-4

- Womick, J., Eckelkamp, J., Luzzo, S., Ward, S. J., Baker, S. G., Salamun, A., & King, L. A. (2021). *Exposure to authoritarian values leads to lower positive affect, higher negative affect, and higher meaning in life. PLoS ONE*, 16(9). https://doi.org/10.1371/journal.pone.0256759

- Council on Foreign Relations. (2017). *Excerpt: Pathways to Freedom. Council on Foreign Relations.* Retrieved from https://www.cfr.org/excerpt-pathways-freedom

- Cuffley, A. (2022). *Social Media Misinformation and the Prevention of Political Instability and Mass Atrocities. Stimson Center.* Retrieved from https://www.stimson.org/2022/social-media-misinformation-and-the-prevention-of-political-instability-and-mass-atrocities/

- Freedom House. (2022). *The Global Expansion of Authoritarian Rule.* Freedom House. Retrieved from https://freedomhouse.org/report/freedom-world/2022/global-expansion-authoritarian-rule

- Freedom House. (2022). *The global expansion of authoritarian rule*. Freedom House. Retrieved from https://freedomhouse.org/report/freedom-world/2022/global-expansion-authoritarian-rule

- Little, W. (2014). *Chapter 17. Government and Politics. Introduction to Sociology - 1st Canadian Edition*. BCcampus. https://opentextbc.ca/introductiontosociology/chapter/chapter-17-government-and-politics/

- National Endowment for Democracy. (2018). *Issue Brief: How Disinformation Impacts Politics and Publics. NATIONAL ENDOWMENT FOR DEMOCRACY*. Retrieved from https://www.ned.org/issue-brief-how-disinformation-impacts-politics-and-publics/

- Osborne, D., Costello, T. H., Duckitt, J., & Sibley, C. G. (2023). *The psychological causes and societal consequences of authoritarianism. Nature Reviews Psychology*, 2(4), 220-232. https://doi.org/10.1038/s44159-023-00161-4

- Pira, F. (2023). *Disinformation a problem for democracy: profiling and risks of consensus manipulation. Frontiers in Sociology*, 8(10), doi:10.3389/fsoc.2023.1150753

- Protect Democracy. (2024). *The Authoritarian Playbook*. Protect Democracy. Retrieved from https://protectdemocracy.org/work/the-authoritarian-playbook/

- Schnelle, C., Baier, D., Hadjar, A., & Boehnke, K. (2021). *Authoritarianism Beyond Disposition: A Literature Review of Research on Contextual Antecedents. Frontiers in Psychology*, 12. https://doi.org/10.3389/fpsyg.2021.676093

- Schnelle, C., Baier, D., Hadjar, A., & Boehnke, K. (2021). *Authoritarianism Beyond Disposition: A Literature Review of Research on Contextual Antecedents. Frontiers in Psychology*, 12. https://doi.org/10.3389/fpsyg.2021.676093

- Balasubramaniam, R. R. (2009). *Judicial politics in authoritarian regimes. The University of Toronto Law Journal*, 59(3), 405-415. https://www.jstor.org/stable/40542316

- Bateman, S. (2022). *Denying Support for Chinese and China-Enabled Authoritarianism and Repression - U.S.-China Technological "Decoupling": A Strategy and Policy Framework*. Carnegie Endowment for International Peace. Retrieved from https://carnegieendowment.org/2022/04/25/denying-support-for-chinese-and-china-enabled-authoritarianism-and-repression-pub-86924

- Freedom House. (2022). *The Global Expansion of Authoritarian Rule*. Retrieved from

https://freedomhouse.org/report/freedom-world/202
2/global-expansion-authoritarian-rule

- Freedom House. (2022). *The Global Expansion of Authoritarian Rule*. Retrieved from https://freedomhouse.org/report/freedom-world/202 2/global-expansion-authoritarian-rule

- Freedom House. (n.d.). *Countering Authoritarianism*. Retrieved from https://freedomhouse.org/issues/countering-authoritarianism](https://freedomhouse.org/issues/countering-authoritarianism)

- Königs, P. (2022). *Government Surveillance, Privacy, and Legitimacy. Philosophy & Technology*, 35(1), 1-22. https://doi.org/10.1007/s13347-022-00503-9

- Lamensch, M. (2021). *Authoritarianism has been reinvented for the digital age. Centre for International Governance Innovation*. Retrieved from https://www.cigionline.org/articles/authoritarianism-has-been-reinvented-for-the-digital-age/

- Marx, G. T. (n.d.). *Centralization and Security*. Retrieved from https://web.mit.edu/gtmarx/www/cenandsec.html

- Olaniran, B., & Williams, I. (2020). *Social media effects: Hijacking democracy and civility in civic engagement. Platforms, Protests, and the Challenge of Networked Democracy*, 77, 10-28. https://doi.org/10.1007/978-3-030-36525-7_5

- Protect Democracy. (2022). *The Authoritarian Playbook. Protect Democracy.* Retrieved from https://protectdemocracy.org/work/the-authoritarian-playbook/

- Solomon, P. H. Jr. (2007). *Courts and Judges in Authoritarian Regimes. World Politics*, 60(1), 122-145. https://www.jstor.org/stable/40060183

- UNESCO. (2023). *Threats to freedom of press: Violence, disinformation & censorship.* UNESCO. Retrieved from https://www.unesco.org/en/threats-freedom-press-violence-disinformation-censorship

- Binsawad, M., Abbasi, G. A., & Sohaib, O. (2022). *People's expectations and experiences of big data collection in the Saudi context. PeerJ Computer Science*, 8(10). https://doi.org/10.7717/peerj-cs.926

- Freedom House. (2018). *The Rise of Digital Authoritarianism.* Freedom House. Retrieved from https://freedomhouse.org/report/freedom-net/2018/rise-digital-authoritarianism

- Freedom House. (2023). *The repressive power of artificial intelligence*. Freedom on the Net 2023. Retrieved from https://freedomhouse.org/report/freedom-net/2023/repressive-power-artificial-intelligence

- Friends of Europe. (2023). *The end of privacy? From danger to democracy to endangered personal autonomy*. Friends of Europe. Retrieved from https://www.friendsofeurope.org/insights/the-end-of-privacy-from-danger-to-democracy-to-endangered-personal-autonomy/

- Kreko, P. (2017). *The authoritarian capture of social media*. Power 3.0: Understanding Modern Authoritarian Influence. https://www.power3point0.org/2017/11/29/the-authoritarian-capture-of-social-media/

- National Academies of Sciences, Engineering, and Medicine, Division of Behavioral and Social Sciences and Education, Committee on National Statistics, & Citro, C. F. (2017). *Practice 7: Respect for the Privacy and Autonomy of Data Providers*. National Academies Press (US). https://www.ncbi.nlm.nih.gov/books/NBK447395/

- Panditharatne, M. (2023). *How AI Puts Elections at Risk — And the Needed Safeguards*. Brennan Center for Justice. Retrieved from https://www.brennancenter.org/our-work/analysis-opinion/how-ai-puts-elections-risk-and-needed-safeguards

- Parsons, L. (2019). *Harvard professor says surveillance capitalism is undermining democracy. Harvard Gazette.* Retrieved from https://news.harvard.edu/gazette/story/2019/03/harvard-professor-says-surveillance-capitalism-is-undermining-democracy/

- Sekalala, S., Dagron, S., Forman, L., & Meier, B. M. (2020). *Analyzing the Human Rights Impact of Increased Digital Public Health Surveillance during the COVID-19 Crisis. Health and Human Rights,* 22(7). Retrieved from https://www.ncbi.nlm.nih.gov/pmc/articles/PMC7762901/

- Wirtschafter, V. (2024). *The impact of generative AI in a global election year.* Brookings. Retrieved from https://www.brookings.edu/articles/the-impact-of-generative-ai-in-a-global-election-year/

- Yayboke, E., & Brannen, S. (2020). *Promote and Build: A Strategic Approach to Digital Authoritarianism.* Center for Strategic and International Studies. Retrieved from https://www.csis.org/analysis/promote-and-build-strategic-approach-digital-authoritarianism

- American Civil Liberties Union. (2022). *Privacy and Surveillance.* Retrieved from https://www.aclu.org/issues/national-security/privacy-and-surveillance

- Auxier, B., Rainie, L., Anderson, M., Perrin, A., Kumar, M., & Turner, E. (2019). *Americans and Privacy: Concerned, Confused and Feeling Lack of Control Over Their Personal Information. Pew Research Center.* https://www.pewresearch.org/internet/2019/11/15/americans-and-privacy-concerned-confused-and-feeling-lack-of-control-over-their-personal-information/

- Harvard Business Review. (2022). *The new rules of data privacy.* Retrieved from https://hbr.org/2022/02/the-new-rules-of-data-privacy

- Harvard Business Review. (2023). *The devastating business impacts of a cyber breach.* Cybersecurity and digital privacy. Retrieved from https://hbr.org/2023/05/the-devastating-business-impacts-of-a-cyber-breach

- IEEE Digital Privacy. (n.d.). *Ethical issues related to data privacy and security: Why we must balance ethical and legal requirements in the connected world.* https://digitalprivacy.ieee.org/publications/topics/ethical-issues-related-to-data-privacy-and-security-why-

- we-must-balance-ethical-and-legal-requirements-in-the-connected-world

- ISACA. (2016). *An ethical approach to data privacy protection. ISACA Journal*, 6. https://www.isaca.org/resources/isaca-journal/issues/2016/volume-6/an-ethical-approach-to-data-privacy-protection

- Lee, N. T., & Chin, C. (2022). *Police surveillance and facial recognition: Why data privacy is imperative for communities of color.* Brookings. Retrieved from https://www.brookings.edu/articles/police-surveillance-and-facial-recognition-why-data-privacy-is-an-imperative-for-communities-of-color/

- Levinson-Waldman, R., Panduranga, H., & Patel, F. (2022). *Social media surveillance by the U.S. government.* Brennan Center for Justice. Retrieved from https://www.brennancenter.org/our-work/research-reports/social-media-surveillance-us-government

- Morey, T., Forbath, J., & Schoop, A. (2015). *Customer data: Designing for transparency and trust. Harvard Business Review.* https://hbr.org/2015/05/customer-data-designing-for-transparency-and-trust

- Seven Pillars Institute. (2021). *Case Study: Equifax Data Breach.* Seven Pillars Institute.

- https://sevenpillarsinstitute.org/case-study-equifax-data-breach/

- Véliz, C. (2021). *Privacy and digital ethics after the pandemic. Nature Electronics*, 4(1), 10-11. https://doi.org/10.1038/s41928-020-00536-y

- Freedom House. (2022). *The Global Expansion of Authoritarian Rule.* Freedom House. Retrieved from https://freedomhouse.org/report/freedom-world/2022/global-expansion-authoritarian-rule

- Freedom House. (2022). *The Global Expansion of Authoritarian Rule.* Retrieved from https://freedomhouse.org/report/freedom-world/2022/global-expansion-authoritarian-rule

- Freedom House. (2022). *The global expansion of authoritarian rule.* Freedom House. https://freedomhouse.org/report/freedom-world/2022/global-expansion-authoritarian-rule

- IFES. (n.d.). *Understanding and interrupting authoritarian collaboration: Stigmatization.* https://www.ifes.org/understanding-and-interrupting-authoritarian-collaboration/stigmatization

- International Republican Institute. (n.d.). *Countering Foreign Authoritarian Influence.* Retrieved from https://www.iri.org/what-we-do/countering-foreign-authoritarian-influence/

- Kleinfeld, R. (2023). *Polarization, Democracy, and Political Violence in the United States: What the Research Says*. Carnegie Endowment for International Peace. Retrieved from https://carnegieendowment.org/2023/09/05/polarization-democracy-and-political-violence-in-united-states-what-research-says-pub-90457

- National Endowment for Democracy. (2020). *A Strategy for Democratic Renewal: Meeting the Challenges Ahead*. NATIONAL ENDOWMENT FOR DEMOCRACY. Retrieved from https://www.ned.org/a-strategy-for-democratic-renewal-meeting-the-challenges-ahead/

- Odora, A. F. (2008). *Rising from the Ashes: The Rebirth of Civil Society in an Authoritarian Political Environment. The International Journal of Not-for-Profit Law*, 10(3). https://www.icnl.org/resources/research/ijnl/rising-from-the-ashes-the-rebirth-of-civil-society-in-an-authoritarian-political-environment

- Padilha, S. (2017). *Human rights for all: from the struggle against authoritarianism to the construction of an all-inclusive democracy. Sur - International Journal on Human Rights*. Retrieved from https://sur.conectas.org/en/human-rights-struggle-authoritarianism-construction-inclusive-democracy/

- Salamey, I., & Pearson, F. S. (2012). *The Collapse of Middle Eastern Authoritarianism: breaking the barriers of fear and power. Third World Quarterly*, 33(5), 931-948. https://www.jstor.org/stable/41507214

- Wienkoop, N.-K., & Bertrand, E. (2018). *Popular resistance to authoritarian consolidation in Burkina Faso.* Carnegie Endowment for International Peace. Retrieved from https://carnegieendowment.org/2018/05/16/popular-resistance-to-authoritarian-consolidation-in-burkina-faso-pub-76363

- Wikipedia contributors. (n.d.). *Resistance movement.* Wikipedia. Retrieved from https://en.wikipedia.org/wiki/Resistance_movement

- Anderson, D. (2020). *Many tech experts say digital disruption will hurt democracy. Today at Elon.* Retrieved from https://www.elon.edu/u/news/2020/02/21/many-tech-experts-say-digital-disruption-will-hurt-democracy/

- Anderson, J., & Rainie, L. (2020). *Concerns about democracy in the digital age.* Pew Research Center. Retrieved from https://www.pewresearch.org/internet/2020/02/21/concerns-about-democracy-in-the-digital-age/

- Auxier, B., & Rainie, L. (2019). *Key takeaways on Americans' views about privacy, surveillance and data-sharing*. Pew Research Center. Retrieved from https://www.pewresearch.org/short-reads/2019/11/15/key-takeaways-on-americans-views-about-privacy-surveillance-and-data-sharing/

- Brookings. (2023). *Big Tech won. Now what?*. *Brookings*. Retrieved from https://www.brookings.edu/articles/big-tech-won-now-what/

- Dayen, D. (2023). *Big Tech Lobbyists Explain How They Took Over Washington*. *The American Prospect*. Retrieved from https://prospect.org/power/2023-04-18-big-tech-lobbyists-took-over-washington/

- Königs, P. (2022). *Government Surveillance, Privacy, and Legitimacy*. *Philosophy & Technology*, 35(1), 1-22. https://doi.org/10.1007/s13347-022-00503-9

- Proceedings of the National Academy of Sciences. (2022). *Cookie absent*. Proceedings of the National Academy of Sciences. https://www.pnas.org/doi/full/10.1073/pnas.2210666120

- United Nations Human Rights Office. (2021). *Moderating online content: fighting harm or silencing dissent?*. Retrieved from https://www.ohchr.org/en/stories/2021/07/moderating-online-content-fighting-harm-or-silencing-dissent

- Walter, J. (2020). *Content moderation is not synonymous with censorship. Public Knowledge.* Retrieved from https://publicknowledge.org/content-moderation-is-not-synonymous-with-censorship/

- Wheeler, T. (2022). *The tragedy of tech companies: Getting the regulation they want. Brookings.* Retrieved from https://www.brookings.edu/articles/the-tragedy-of-tech-companies-getting-the-regulation-they-want/

- Columbia University Teachers College. (2021). *Information overload: Combating misinformation with critical thinking.* CENTER FOR THE PROFESSIONAL EDUCATION OF TEACHERS. Retrieved from http://cpet.tc.columbia.edu/8/post/2021/04/information-overload-combating-misinformation-with-critical-thinking.html

- Flores, W., & Samuel, J. (2019). *Accelerating action on sustainable development goals: Grassroots organisations and the sustainable development goals: no one left behind?. The BMJ*, 365. https://doi.org/10.1136/bmj.l2269

- Freedom House. (2019). *Policy recommendations: Internet freedom.* Freedom House. Retrieved from https://freedomhouse.org/policy-recommendations/internet-freedom

- Ginsburg, T. (2020). *Authoritarian International Law?*. *American Journal of International Law, 114*(2), 221-260. https://doi.org/10.1017/ajil.2020.3

- Good Party. (n.d.). *The Power of Grassroots Movements in Political Change.* Retrieved from https://goodparty.org/blog/article/grassroots-movement

- Grimshaw, A. (2016). *Putting Democracy Back into Public Education. The Century Foundation.* Retrieved from https://tcf.org/content/report/putting-democracy-back-public-education/

- Julien, H. (2021). *Q&A: New urgency of digital literacy and the fight against misinformation. University at Buffalo Magazine.* Retrieved from https://ed.buffalo.edu/magazine/issues/spring-2021/new-digital-literacy.html

- Penn Today. (n.d.). *Higher education's role in democracy.* Retrieved from https://penntoday.upenn.edu/news/higher-educations-role-democracy

- Principles of Democracy. (n.d.). *Education and Democracy — Principles of Democracy.* Retrieved from https://www.principlesofdemocracy.org/education-dem

- Sloan, M. (n.d.). *Study: Digital literacy doesn't stop the spread of misinformation. MIT Sloan.* Retrieved from https://mitsloan.mit.edu/ideas-made-to-matter/study-digital-literacy-doesnt-stop-spread-misinformation

- UNHCR Innovation. (2019). *Grassroots organizations are just as important as seed money for innovation. UNHCR Innovation.* Retrieved from https://www.unhcr.org/innovation/grassroots-organizations-are-just-as-important-as-seed-money-for-innovation/

- American Psychological Association. (2019). *The legacy of trauma.* Monitor on Psychology. Retrieved from https://www.apa.org/monitor/2019/02/legacy-trauma.

- Asim, M., Zhiying, L., Nadeem, M. A., Ghani, U., Arshad, M., & Yi, X. (2021). *How authoritarian leadership affects employee's helping behavior? The mediating role of rumination and moderating role of psychological ownership. Frontiers in Psychology,* 12, 10.3389/fpsyg.2021.667348. https://doi.org/10.3389/fpsyg.2021.667348

- Harrington, J. R., Boski, P., & Gelfand, M. J. (2015). *Culture and National Well-Being: Should Societies Emphasize Freedom or Constraint?. PLoS ONE,* 10(6), 10.1371/journal.pone.0127173. https://doi.org/10.1371/journal.pone.0127173

- Jiang, H., Chen, Y., Sun, P., & Yang, J. (2017). *The relationship between authoritarian leadership and employees' deviant workplace behaviors: The mediating effects of psychological contract violation and organizational cynicism. Frontiers in Psychology,* 8(10), 10.3389/fpsyg.2017.00732. https://doi.org/10.3389/fpsyg.2017.00732

- Maercker, A. (2023). *How to deal with the past? How collective and historical trauma psychologically reverberates in Eastern Europe. Frontiers in Psychiatry,* 14, article e1228785. https://doi.org/10.3389/fpsyt.2023.1228785

- McCarthy-Jones, S. (2019). *The autonomous mind: The right to freedom of thought in the twenty-first century. Frontiers in Artificial Intelligence,* 2(10). https://doi.org/10.3389/frai.2019.00019

- Osborne, D., Costello, T. H., Duckitt, J., & Sibley, C. G. (2023). *The psychological causes and societal consequences of authoritarianism. Nature Reviews Psychology,* 4(2), 220. https://doi.org/10.1038/s44159-023-00161-4

- Ramalisa, R. J., du Plessis, E., & Koen, M. P. (2018). *Increasing coping and strengthening resilience in nurses providing mental health care: Empirical qualitative research. Health SA = SA Gesondheid,* 23(10). https://doi.org/10.4102/hsag.v23i0.1094

- Wang, Z., Liu, Y., & Liu, S. (2019). *Authoritarian leadership and task performance: The effects of leader-member exchange and dependence on leader. Frontiers of Business Research in China*, 13(1), 1-15. https://doi.org/10.1186/s11782-019-0066-x

- Yayboke, E., & Brannen, S. (2020). *Promote and Build: A Strategic Approach to Digital Authoritarianism.* Retrieved from https://www.csis.org/analysis/promote-and-build-strategic-approach-digital-authoritarianism

- Afoaku, O. G. (2000). *U.S. foreign policy and authoritarian regimes: Change and continuity in international clientelism. Journal of Third World Studies*, 17(2), 13-40. https://www.jstor.org/stable/45198191

- Carothers, T., & Feldman, B. (2024). *Examining U.S. Relations With Authoritarian Countries.* Carnegie Endowment for International Peace. Retrieved from https://carnegieendowment.org/2023/12/13/examining-u.s.-relations-with-authoritarian-countries-pub-91231

- Chien, C.-L. (2016). *Beyond authoritarian personality: The culture-inclusive theory of chinese authoritarian orientation. Frontiers in Psychology,* 7, Article 924. https://doi.org/10.3389/fpsyg.2016.00924

- Fell, A. (2024). *How Autocrats Control Internet Traffic Out of Sight. PNAS Nexus.* https://www.ucdavis.edu/curiosity/news/how-autocrats-control-internet-traffic-out-sight

- Freedom House. (2022). *The Global Expansion of Authoritarian Rule.* Freedom House. Retrieved from https://freedomhouse.org/report/freedom-world/2022/global-expansion-authoritarian-rule

- Freedom House. (2022). *The Global Expansion of Authoritarian Rule.* Retrieved from https://freedomhouse.org/report/freedom-world/2022/global-expansion-authoritarian-rule

- Freedom House. (2022). *The global expansion of authoritarian rule.* Retrieved from https://freedomhouse.org/report/freedom-world/2022/global-expansion-authoritarian-rule

- Lamensch, M. (2021). *Authoritarianism has been reinvented for the digital age.* Centre for International Governance Innovation. Retrieved from https://www.cigionline.org/articles/authoritarianism-has-been-reinvented-for-the-digital-age/

- Raderstorf, B. (2022). *The Authoritarian Playbook. Protect Democracy.* Retrieved from https://protectdemocracy.org/work/the-authoritarian-playbook/

- Schnelle, C., Baier, D., Hadjar, A., & Boehnke, K. (2021). *Authoritarianism Beyond Disposition: A Literature Review of Research on Contextual Antecedents. Frontiers in Psychology*, 12. https://doi.org/10.3389/fpsyg.2021.676093

- Walker, J. (2023). *The world has become flatter for authoritarian regimes. Journal of Democracy.* https://www.journalofdemocracy.org/online-exclusive/the-world-has-become-flatter-for-authoritarian-regimes/

- Wikipedia contributors. (n.d.). *Authoritarianism. Wikipedia*. Retrieved from https://en.wikipedia.org/wiki/Authoritarianism.

- Brennan Center for Justice. (n.d.). *Policy Solutions*. https://www.brennancenter.org/our-work/policy-solutions

- Brookings Institution. (2013). *Democracy, Human Rights and the Emerging Global Order*. Retrieved from https://www.brookings.edu/articles/democracy-human-rights-and-the-emerging-global-order/

- CIRCLE. (n.d.). *Why Is Youth Civic Engagement Important?*. Retrieved from https://circle.tufts.edu/index.php/understanding-youth-civic-engagement/why-it-important

- Freedom House. (2019). *Policy Recommendations: Internet Freedom*. Freedom House. Retrieved from https://freedomhouse.org/policy-recommendations/internet-freedom

- Freedom House. (2020). *Principles for safeguarding US democracy*. Retrieved from https://freedomhouse.org/article/principles-safeguarding-us-democracy

- Ginsberg, H. (n.d.). *Civic and democratic engagement: A brief overview*. Retrieived from https://ginsberg.umich.edu/article/civic-and-democratic-engagement-brief-overview

- ISACA. (2023). *The role of transparency and accountability in digital transformation*. ISACA News and Trends. Retrieved from https://www.isaca.org/resources/news-and-trends/industry-news/2023/the-role-of-transparency-and-accountability-in-digital-transformation

- Making All Voices Count. (n.d.). *Technologies for transparency and accountability Archives - Making All Voices Count*. Retrieved from https://www.makingallvoicescount.org/topic/technologies-for-transparency-and-accountability/

- Office of the United Nations High Commissioner for Human Rights. (n.d.). *International standards*.

Retrieved from https://www.ohchr.org/en/special-procedures/ie-foreign-debt/international-standards

- Open Government Partnership. (2021). *Actions for Transparent and Accountable Digital Governance.* Open Government Partnership. Retrieved from https://www.opengovpartnership.org/actions-for-transparent-and-accountable-digital-governance/

- The Policy Circle. (n.d.). *Civic Engagement - What is civic engagement?.* Retrieved from https://www.thepolicycircle.org/brief/whats-whys-civic-engagement/

- Freedom House. (2022). *The Global Expansion of Authoritarian Rule.* Retrieved from https://freedomhouse.org/report/freedom-world/2022/global-expansion-authoritarian-rule

- Parliamentarians for Global Action. (2024). *Erosion of democratic principles.* Parliamentarians for Global Action. Retrieved from https://www.pgaction.org/dgi/drhr/parliamentary-toolbox-for-democracy-defense/erosion-of-democratic-principles.html

- Williamson, V. (2023). *Understanding democratic decline in the United States. Brookings.* Retrieved from https://www.brookings.edu/articles/understanding-democratic-decline-in-the-united-states/

www.ingramcontent.com/pod-product-compliance
Lightning Source LLC
Chambersburg PA
CBHW061628250726
48659CB00004B/1121